'Making It' as a Contract Researcher

'Making It' as a Contract Researcher examines the contemporary experience of research employment in universities from the perspective of a significant yet often invisible group: temporary or contract researchers, who make up a substantial, and ever-growing, proportion of the academic research workforce. A critical, pragmatic and international account of the contemporary research career, this book explores the question of what it means to 'make it' as a contract researcher in academia, and how individuals and organisations in higher education might seek to do things differently.

Providing the reader with practical and realistic strategies for improving the experience of being a contract researcher and achieving and sustaining an academic research career, this book guides the reader on a range of topics, including:

- Charging fairly for your work
- Building a publication track record
- Finding the next contract
- Sustaining your network
- Feeling like you belong
- Moving beyond contract research.

Using a combination of current research, interviews and reflective writing, the book is written specifically for and by contract researchers in academia, offering unique and extremely valuable advice for all new and current contract researchers, including PhD students, early career researchers and any party interested in pursuing a research career in academia.

Nerida Spina is a senior lecturer at the Queensland University of Technology, Australia.

Jess Harris is an associate professor at the University of Newcastle, Australia.

Simon Bailey is a research associate at the University of Kent, UK.

Mhorag Goff is a research associate at the University of Manchester, UK.

Insider Guides to Success in Academia
Series Editors:
Helen Kara,
Independent Researcher, UK and
Pat Thomson,
The University of Nottingham, UK

The *Insiders' Guides to Success in Academia* address topics too small for a full-length book on their own, but too big to cover in a single chapter or article. These topics have often been the stuff of discussions on social media, or of questions in our workshops. We designed this series to answer these questions and to provide practical support for doctoral and early career researchers. It is geared to concerns that many people experience. Readers will find these books to be companions that provide advice and help to make sense of everyday life in the contemporary university.

We have therefore:

(1) invited scholars with deep and specific expertise to write. Our writers use their research and professional experience to provide well-grounded strategies to particular situations.
(2) asked writers to collaborate. Most of the books are produced by writers who live in different countries, or work in different disciplines, or both. While it is difficult for any book to cover all the diverse contexts in which potential readers live and work, the different perspectives and contexts of writers goes some way to address this problem.

We understand that the use of the term 'academia' might be read as meaning the university, but we take a broader view. Pat does indeed work in a university, but spent a long time working outside of one. Helen is an independent researcher and sometimes works with universities. Both of us understand academic – or scholarly – work as now being conducted in a range of sites, from museums and the public sector to industry research and development laboratories. Academic work is also often undertaken by networks that bring together scholars in various locations. All of our writers understand that this is the case, and use the term 'academic' in this wider sense.

These books are pocket sized so that they can be carried around and visited again and again. Most of the books have a mix of examples, stories and exercises as well as explanation and advice. They are written in a collegial tone, and from a position of care as well as knowledge.

Together with our writers, we hope that each book in the series can make a positive contribution to the work and life of readers, so that you too can become insiders in scholarship.

Helen Kara, PhD FAcSS,
independent researcher
https://helenkara.com/
@DrHelenKara (Twitter/Insta)
Pat Thomson PhD PSM FAcSS FRSA
Professor of Education, The University of Nottingham
https://patthomson.net
@ThomsonPat

Books in the Series:

Publishing from your Doctoral Research
Create and Use a Publication Strategy
Janet Salmons and Helen Kara

'Making It' as a Contract Researcher
A Pragmatic Look at Precarious Work
Nerida Spina, Jess Harris, Simon Bailey and Mhorag Goff

'Making It' as a Contract Researcher

A Pragmatic Look at Precarious Work

Nerida Spina, Jess Harris, Simon Bailey and Mhorag Goff

LONDON AND NEW YORK

First published 2020
by Routledge
2 Park Square, Milton Park, Abingdon, Oxon OX14 4RN

and by Routledge
52 Vanderbilt Avenue, New York, NY 10017

Routledge is an imprint of the Taylor & Francis Group, an informa business

© 2020 Nerida Spina, Jess Harris, Simon Bailey and Mhorag Goff

The right of Nerida Spina, Jess Harris, Simon Bailey and Mhorag Goff to be identified as authors of this work has been asserted by them in accordance with sections 77 and 78 of the Copyright, Designs and Patents Act 1988.

All rights reserved. No part of this book may be reprinted or reproduced or utilised in any form or by any electronic, mechanical, or other means, now known or hereafter invented, including photocopying and recording, or in any information storage or retrieval system, without permission in writing from the publishers.

Trademark notice: Product or corporate names may be trademarks or registered trademarks, and are used only for identification and explanation without intent to infringe.

British Library Cataloguing-in-Publication Data
A catalogue record for this book is available from the British Library

Library of Congress Cataloging-in-Publication Data
A catalog record has been requested for this book

ISBN: 978-1-138-36258-1 (hbk)
ISBN: 978-1-138-36259-8 (pbk)
ISBN: 978-0-429-43199-9 (ebk)

Typeset in Helvetica
by Swales & Willis, Exeter, Devon, UK

Contents

Preface	x
Acknowledgements	xvi
1 Situating the contract research career	**1**
The partial academic	1
What is *making it*?	2
Introduction to the research	4
Some key terms	6
Who is this book for?	7
How this book is organised	9
Chapter 1: situating the contract research career	9
Chapter 2: becoming and being a contract researcher	10
Chapter 3: the collective work of contract research	11
Chapter 4: the possible future of research careers	11
What is work?	12
The growth of contract research	13
Who are contract researchers?	17
Policy context	22
Feeling the effects of managerialism	24
Consequences for researchers	26
A final word	29
Note	30
References	30

2 Becoming and being a contract researcher — 37
The multiplicity of *making it* — 37
    Entry into contract research — 38
Progressing as a contract researcher — 43
    Developing the academic identity — 44
    Being strategic and developing your research story — 49
    Building a publication track record — 55
    Acquiring in-demand skills — 57
    Managing quality research — 60
The hidden work of a contract researcher — 62
    Charging fairly for your work — 68
    Finding the next contract — 72
    Managing periods of under or unemployment — 73
    Health, ageing and contract research — 78
Moving beyond contract research — 86
    Tenured academic job applications — 88
    Moving to non-research positions — 91
A final word — 93
Notes — 98
References — 98

3 The collective work of contract research — 102
Collegiality, not competition — 102
Employment on other people's projects — 104
    Quality research: balancing independence and collegiality — 107
    Ethical dilemmas — 111
    Feeling like you belong — 114
    Writing on other people's projects — 115
    Working for free — 118
    Questions of authorship — 121
    Initiating publications in a team — 125
The collective work of career building — 127
    Creating and maintaining your networks — 127

Sustaining your network	131
Conferences and professional organisations	139
Networks of contract researchers	141
Collectivisation among researchers	144
A final word	150
Note	151
References	151

4 The possible future of research careers **154**
Nurturing engagement	154
Supporting contract researchers to *make it*	155
Individual efforts	158
Group work: collectivisation among researchers	158
Supervisory action and ethical leadership	160
Industrial action: the role of unions and activism	170
Research associations	172
The impact of institutional initiatives	174
Impacts on universities	177
Government-led reform	180
A final word	182
Notes	183
References	184

Index 187

Preface

The strike[1] has certainly surfaced some tensions. I'm cynical about strikes in any case, but a couple of things I've reflected upon with the current 'radical' strike action: withdrawing my work from the university does not have the same impact as a lecturer withdrawing their work, as I do not have classes to teach or students to look after.

There will be no inconvenience to the university even in the short term because work will be made up by people working harder or for longer to achieve the same goals. The wider institutional structure of research will be unaffected by me withdrawing my work—if research is delayed the costs for this delay will be borne by individual project teams through uncosted extensions.

If I withdraw my work entirely, then I will not make various deadlines. Some of these are non-negotiable. Some of them carry weighty personal investments of time, e.g. resubmission deadlines. Taking a 14 day pay cut will require me to borrow money in order to get through the month. My conclusion is that the main person to be inconvenienced by me withdrawing my work is me!

> Therefore, I have exercised my right to solidarity, I will not cross a picket line, but I'm not striking. My pension is, of course, equally at risk as everyone else's.
> —Reflections of a contract researcher

This book examines the contemporary experience of research employment in universities from the perspective of a significant yet often invisible group: the temporary or contract researchers who make up a substantial proportion of the academic research workforce. While substantial research attention has been paid to issues related to sessional academic teaching (e.g. Bryson 2013; Klopper & Power 2014; Percy & Beaumont 2008; Ryan, Burgess, Connell & Groen 2013), there has been little discussion of the experiences of temporary research staff. The discussion may well be quite familiar to you, if you have experience working in universities or other research institutes. However, we believe that the current situation, which we will discuss in greater depth throughout the book, is different from the past. First, the number of people employed on temporary contracts as a proportion of the total academic research workforce has soared; second, and partly as a consequence of the first point, contract research has become an academic career trajectory, whereas in the past it was considered a stepping stone to something else; and third, academic employment has not been immune from wider trends towards casual and insecure employment (e.g. Standing, 2011) impacting experiences of 'permanence' and 'tenure', with the image of homo academicus, if it existed at all, now only experienced by a very small minority. We therefore hope to contribute to the conversations on the changing nature of research and employment that have occurred over recent decades in advanced liberal democracies. The substantial increase in temporary employment is one of these changes, and is symptomatic of broader shifts towards efficiency and measurability. We believe universities have reached a tipping point where a large proportion of the research workforce are insecurely employed. We are only now beginning to collectively recognise the impact that this shift has on the lived experiences of those researchers, and these are the issues to which we would like to draw attention.

The dependence of universities and research institutes on casual and temporary forms of employment has become a very ordinary state of affairs. Our intention is to disrupt this ordinariness so we might begin to think differently. We know much of what we have documented is discussed informally among researchers on a regular basis. Dramatic growth in academic 'quit lit' (e.g. Pryal 2018) parallels the growth in contract research, as the number of highly qualified researchers has outgrown the number of academic positions available. We recognise that there are many researchers working on contracts outside the academy, in government organisations, think-tanks, research institutions and as independent scholars. This book is primarily targeted at sharing the experiences contract researchers in academia, though it is possible that the narratives presented herein may resonate with those outside the academy.

Many of the issues faced by contract researchers in academia remain hidden from view. Evidence from our own research and from the literature demonstrates that those who are most affected do not want to be seen to complain and risk their current or future employment. Although it is a complex and often troubling environment, we are encouraged by the increasing attention to these realities in public discourse, and through newspapers, blogs and other social media. We welcome this trend and see our contribution as an extension of it—bringing this informal and somewhat hidden knowledge further into the light, and asking what might be done about it: how can the institutions and those therein best recognise and support contract researchers?

This book started out as a blog, or rather, a small series of blogs, initiated by Professor Pat Thomson on her popular blog: https://patthomson.net/. The post featured an introductory piece by Pat followed by four guest commentaries on the subject of 'working on other people's projects'. Nerida and Jess wrote one of these commentaries together, Simon wrote another. At that time, Mhorag and Simon were working in the same university and were involved in some researcher development activities, and so began a conversation. This conversation became part of another, when Pat suggested we put something together for a series of short books she was proposing based upon insider accounts of academia.

Between the four of us, we have almost 40 years' experience of working on temporary contracts and on other people's projects. As part of the research for this book we have spoken to many more people. Our collective experiences are diverse and situated by a variety of national and institutional contexts. Yet across this diversity there is also coherence around a number of matters of concern, which we examine in the following pages.

It wasn't until we began the work of putting together a proposal that we realised how little has been published that is devoted to contract research and the experience of contract researchers. While there has been increasing recognition of teaching casualisation in the academy, less has been said about the research workforce. We recognise that there are substantial issues faced by temporary teaching academics, often shared by contract researchers. The issues described in this book, however, focus on those who are undertaking research work for temporary or fixed-term periods in universities. We also acknowledge that many people undertake both teaching and research contracts simultaneously and have included their stories because of the significant impact on their research careers.

To the best of our knowledge this is the first book written by and for contract researchers that examines their experiences and the wider conditions that shape them. We are forever grateful to the incredibly open and candid researchers who contributed their time and experiences to this project, through interviews, hallway or email discussions or through writing their blogs or reflections. Their stories have been incorporated throughout the book on a condition of anonymity. We have used pseudonyms for all participants and deidentified names of institutions, locations, and research groups described in the book as promised to participants. While many of their stories felt familiar and shared key elements, there is much more to be said on this topic than can fit into this book; however, we hope to have played a small part in moving the conversation forward.

Note

1 'The strike' refers to industrial action taken by academics in the UK across 64 universities in 2018. The dispute was centred around proposed changes to superannuation schemes.

References

Bryson, C., 2013, 'Supporting Sessional Teaching Staff in the UK—to What Extent is There Real Progress?' *Journal of University Teaching and Learning Practice*, vol. 10, no. 3, p. 2.

Klopper, C.J., & Power, B. M., 2014, 'The Casual Approach to Teacher Education: What Effect Does Casualisation Have for Australian University Teaching?', *Australian Journal of Teacher Education*, vol. 39, no. 4, p. 4.

Percy, A., & Beaumont, R., 2008, 'The Casualisation of Teaching and the Subject at Risk', *Studies in Continuing Education*, vol. 30, no. 2, pp. 145–157.

Pryal, K.R.G., 2018, 'Quit Lit Is About Labor Conditions', *Women in Higher Education*, vol. 27, no. 6, pp. 1–2.

Ryan, S., Burgess, J., Connell, J., & Groen, E., 2013, 'Casual Academic Staff in an Australian University: Marginalised and Excluded', *Tertiary Education and Management*, vol. 19, no. 2, pp. 161–175.

Standing, G., 2011, *The Precariat: The New Dangerous Class*, London: Bloomsbury Academic.

Acknowledgements

We would like to begin by thanking the researchers who so generously shared their experiences with us and to the original authors of the blog series on https://patthomson.net/, Dr Daniel Sawyer, Dr Emily St Denny, Dr Sharon McCulloch and Dr Teena Clarke. Your stories demonstrate how precarity pervades all aspects of life, including major decisions about finances, health, and family. Your insights and powerful experiences challenged us to think about the significant impact of contract research, on research, careers, and individuals. We have done our very best to represent your stories well, so others might learn from your experiences.

We are extremely grateful to Professor Pat Thomson and Dr Helen Kara, whose interest in the experiences and realities of those in less privileged positions sparked an international conversation and bought us together as authors. We have learned a great deal from our regular online conversations and are thankful for this opportunity. We are also grateful for the generosity of Emeritus Professor Raewyn Connell and Professor Helen Sword who both shared their insights about the changing nature of academic employment. It was immediately obvious to us that you have acted as strong allies for non-tenured colleagues. However imperfectly, we have aimed to build on your contributions in some small way by making a case for strong, ethical leadership. We ourselves have all been fortunate to have been mentored by strong, ethical leaders during our research careers. While we can't name everyone, we would like to thank (in no particular order)

Barbara Comber, Val Klenowski, Suzanne Carrington, Ann Farrell, Jenny Gore, Susan Danby, Brian Caldwell, Carolyn D. Baker, Debra Howcroft, Damian Hodgson, Mel Ainscow, and Kath Checkland.

We have been fortunate to have had some contract researchers work on this book in various capacities. Their work has ranged from finding literature, to writing commentary and commenting on drafts. We thank you for your expertise and time: Dr Helen Breathnach, Dr Alex Jones, Kate Smithers, Sarah Gurr, Kate Bennett, Oz Gore, Sandra Etoka, Sharon McCullough and Teena Clarke. We would also like to acknowledge the support of the *Childhoods in Changing Contexts* Research Group at Queensland University of Technology, who provided funding for some of this research support. A special thank you to Gabby Spina who has undertaken the enormous job of editing this book for us. Bringing together a work such as this into one cohesive volume is no small task—your patience and expertise has been invaluable.

Finally, thank you to all of our families who have put up with strange meeting timings to accommodate international time differences.

1 Situating the contract research career

The partial academic

I recently sat down to read Les Back's (2016) 'Academic Diary'. I remember the anticipation I felt. The book had been recommended to me by a close colleague. I knew enough about the project to feel that this was going to speak to experiences that I had shared in, that it might offer me some playful yet serious critiques of the contemporary academy and some of the everyday realities of the work of knowledge production in which we are all engaged.

Opening the book, I smiled as I realised it was written as 'an academic diary'. Yet almost instantaneously this device caused me to feel a deep sense of disconnection between me and the work. It begins in September, the start of the academic year, and the events and activities it describes move to the rhythms of lectures, semesters, dissertations, exams; guiding students through the rituals of a university education.

But these are not my rhythms and not my rituals. If these are not my rhythms, then this is not my diary. The 'we' that I thought might be more clearly articulated through this work was not the troubled, fractured 'we' that I now feel. Yet here 'we' are occupying the same institutional space, or rather as I now realised, occupying a partially shared space, vis-à-vis 'the academic' and 'the researcher'.

My work moves to the rhythms of projects and contracts. It is polyrhythmic in this sense, and frequently arrhythmic—after all, projects don't end like contracts do. And yet, the struggle in which Back is engaged, the values he holds, and the collective, collegiate practices for which he so passionately argues— these are also my struggles, my values, my passions.

'We' must come to a better understanding with one another if we are to collectively realise these.

—Reflections of a contract researcher

What is *making it*?

I was thinking that when I read the information sheet [about the research] the title 'Making it as a contract researcher', and I thought, what does *making it* mean in this context? And I thought is, *making it* having your name on an [major] grant? Is it having a PhD? Is it just the fact that I've been employed consistently for ten years?

—Laura

Situating the contract research career 3

The notion of *making it* as a contract researcher is fraught. For many of the researchers that we talked to, like Laura, the concept of success means gaining permanent employment within the academy. The evidence is clear, however, that securing ongoing academic employment is increasingly difficult (European University Institute 2019; Petrova 2017; Rea 2015). As ongoing academic positions have become more scarce, candidates are being asked to reach higher targets to secure these positions. Whereas a PhD might once have led to a faculty position, potential employees are now typically expected to have produced high-quality published work, be active contributors to grants and have extensive research (and teaching) experience to get their foot in the door. The intensification of academic work has created a sense that only 'heroic' researchers can move beyond contract work. One of our participants, Emma, said:

> I do want a successful academic career and to get any kind of permanent position, you need to be a superstar and so you need to build yourself up to be that to even get a level B role … I know amazing academics who have won awards and are amazing but can't get anything more than sessional teaching.

In this book, we want to challenge the idea that *making it* as a contract researcher is solely measured by securing an ongoing academic position. Rather, we want to celebrate the talent and skills of researchers who are working in precarious fixed-term or casual positions both within and beyond university settings. The definition of *making it* that we have adopted is that contract researchers are recognised as integral members of a research team, that their contributions are valued by all of their colleagues and their institution and that they are given opportunities to build their knowledge, skills and networks. While we recognise the significant structural issues that underpin many of the ongoing disparities in research employment (particularly in Chapter 4), this book adopts a pragmatic stance in which we seek to support contract researchers who currently work in this context.

Introduction to the research

The value generated by public research is estimated to be between three and eight times its initial investment over its life cycle (Georghiou 2015). Annual rates of return on investment average between 20% and 50%. Within this context it is appropriate to question the extent to which the people generating this value—including researchers employed on fixed-term contracts—are able to translate this work into sustainable and satisfying careers.

The phenomenon of the fixed-term contract researcher has been driven by neoliberal reforms that have transformed universities into 'rational' service organisations (Nadolny et al. 2011). Marketisation and the massification of higher education (Barcan 2013; Macfarlane 2010; Nikolaidis & Maroudas 2013), alongside changes in research funding structures, have reshaped the nature of academic work and employment. Macfarlane (2010, p. 59) has characterised the shift to reducing tenured positions and specialising academic work into either teaching or research functions as a 'silent revolution'. Data from the US (Flaherty 2018) indicates 'contingent'[1] faculty now make up 70% of the academic labour force. In Australia, the number of students attending higher education institutions has tripled over the past three decades, while the proportion of academic staff in continuing positions has declined by almost 20% (Andrews et al. 2016). As we will discuss below, much of the data about university staff conflates teaching and research employment, which can obscure the experiences of those whose primary focus is research.

It is in this landscape that we have produced this book. Alongside a review of the literature and an exploration of policy contexts, we conducted interviews with 29 people, a mixture of researchers and senior academics, and held informal conversations with dozens more in Australia and the UK, with a number having had experience in other countries including New Zealand and North America. An additional three participants offered their views in writing (rather than participating in interviews). Our participants had typically worked in a number of universities and other research settings (such as hospitals, think-tanks and the public services sector). Our interviews were loosely structured allowing participants to tell their individual stories about their experiences of working for universities under precarious employment conditions. We started with the everyday experiences of these researchers as the 'point d'appui' [point of entry] (Smith 2005, p. 10) for a narrative analysis, examining shared experiences of their work within academic institutions. The narrative analysis was informed by our 'insider's perspective', drawing on our own experiences of working on contract in universities. A thematic analysis of interview data was also undertaken to identify specific challenges these precarious researchers face. While we each had our own stories of working as a contract researcher in academia, we were struck by themes related to gender, age, health issues, mobility and family life that emerged through these analyses. Following Floersch et al. (2010), we found that thematic analysis 'allow[ed] us to see patterns in our dataset … and narrative analysis add[ed] temporality and plot' (p. 408). In addition, we have included many of the practical ideas our participants offered around how to navigate, survive—and even thrive—in contemporary research employment.

Some key terms

There are a wide variety of contractual bases for non-tenured researchers that vary substantially between institutions and national settings. Research work ranges from being employed on very short-term casual contracts (sometimes for a few days or under 40 hours) through to full-time fixed-term contracts that might last anywhere between a month and a number of years. In researching and writing this book, we found that while fixed-term appointments of one to three years are more common in UK universities, Australian research work often involves researchers navigating casual employment for short periods across multiple projects and contracts. We provide a more detailed explanation of the categories and modes of employment later in this chapter. We have chosen to use the umbrella term 'contract research' across this book. We use this term to include all modes of employment characterised by a level of insecurity in that they do not offer a guaranteed or obvious path to permanent, ongoing employment.

Who is this book for?

This book is written primarily from the perspectives of social sciences and humanities researchers within universities. While they share many experiences with researchers in STEM subjects, the imagery, narratives and imperatives that dominate STEM research, for example around mobility, can tend to overshadow and elide other experiences, including those of researchers in non-STEM disciplines. Social sciences and humanities researchers are largely absent from most national level policy on research and researchers and likewise in guidance that might support social sciences researchers in developing their careers.

We have imagined the readers of this book might be people embarking on higher degree research and dipping their toes into paid research alongside their studies, researchers who are already employed precariously and those who supervise them. We imagine many of you might be hoping to find out more about how to sustain a long-term career, and perhaps attain ongoing employment. We have listened to the stories of researchers who have been in each of these situations and have written this book with your needs in mind. We want to address the anxieties, tensions and systemic inequalities you may experience. However, we also want to offer some hope, and consider how to navigate precarity in ways that are personally and professionally fulfilling. A core component of this is to think about how researchers might work collectively towards new possibilities. We were fortunate enough to have a conversation with Professor Raewyn Connell as part of this project. She shared her incredible knowledge of life in universities and suggested 'it's a problem that only has collective solutions, not individual ones ... It's not a matter of therapy!' To draw on the words of another esteemed sociologist, Stephen Ball (2015, p. 15):

> The point is that in neoliberal economies, sites of government and points of contact are also sites for the possibility of refusal. However, the starting point for a politics of refusal is the site of subjectivity. It is a struggle over and against what it is we have become, what it is that we do not want to be.

We also hope tenured staff who are interested in understanding the significant challenges non-tenured colleagues face might find this work illuminating. We recognise that tenured staff in universities are not immune from many of the issues outlined in this book. All academic staff are subjected to pressures of workload and balance within the neoliberal institution. The dominant *'publish or perish'* discourse positions all academics, who engage in research, to secure grant funding, produce high-quality research papers, travel to conferences and juggle a demanding workload that extends beyond traditional working hours. Despite these shared challenges, we argue that additional challenges contract researchers must overcome are often hidden from the view of academics in ongoing employment. Little training is available for academics to manage the researchers that they employ to work on projects and publications; however, many of the academics who employ contract researchers want to offer fair and supportive employment conditions. As such, we have included suggestions from our research participants around the informal and formal practices that those in more senior and secure positions can adopt in support of their non-tenured colleagues.

How this book is organised

Each chapter that follows features empirical material drawn from interviews and accounts from contract researchers in a variety of disciplinary contexts, primarily in the social sciences. The vast majority of these interviews are drawn from university settings in Australia and the United Kingdom and provide first-person narratives of current and former contract researchers, with some insight from academics with experience in employing and supervising large teams of contract researchers. These interviews offer insights into the limits and opportunities available in a range of different roles and career paths: from doctoral students and early career researchers, through to senior research fellows. While this work began from the everyday, embodied experiences of real researchers in real places, our goal was to use these important points, problems and possibilities to illuminate the institutional and social conditions in which precarity and marginalisation prosper.

Chapter 1: situating the contract research career

This chapter examines the contemporary research field in advanced liberal democracies. Drawing upon research literature, the chapter situates the rise of contract research careers in the context of broad socio-political trends towards marketisation. These trends have shaped the character of contemporary research careers, making the successive accumulation of temporary contracts a *normal* state of employment for many researchers. In addition to being made vulnerable to exclusion and exploitation, these conditions place contract researchers in an ambiguous and conflicted position *vis-à-vis* the core purpose and wider consequences of their employment. Drawing on secondary quantitative data, this chapter maps the field of contract research, describing the scale, scope and variety of contract research roles across a range of organisational and institutional contexts.

Chapter 2: becoming and being a contract researcher

Chapter 2 describes the most common routes through which individuals become contract researchers. Drawing on discussions with current and former contract researchers, the chapter describes the means, formal and informal, by which researchers' work is arranged and managed. We explore the skills and attributes that are valued, and the work involved in being a contract researcher. This chapter highlights the hidden work that precariously employed researchers must undertake, and the struggles they experience in managing their everyday realities. We conclude with a discussion of possibilities and realities for moving beyond contract research.

Chapter 3: the collective work of contract research

This chapter focuses on the importance of what we have called the *collective work* of research. We outline the importance of developing productive relationships with others who understand and care about you; and are in a position to support your employment and research agenda. We also raise the importance of the informal collectivising strategies, through which contract researchers can collaboratively protect, support and encourage each other. Collectivisation can generate more productive and predictable working conditions; and provide the emotional and practical support systems that are vitally important for those who are employed precariously. We recognise that transformative change requires the support of tenured colleagues, as well as a commitment from the institutions to legitimise, sustain and normalise better employment conditions.

Chapter 4: the possible future of research careers

We conclude with a prospective look at possible means to lift isolated individual strategies, to connect them with organisational policies and practices, and the wider institutional conditions that can better support, develop and sustain a collective sense of belonging for contract researchers. We acknowledge that the take up of these practices is, at best, patchy. As a number of our participants told us, many of the specific challenges of contract research seem to be invisible to institutional and meta-institutional level organising structures. However, we also highlight some instances in which institutions (universities, funding bodies, unions and research organisations) *have* made attempts to redress some of the systemic injustice that subjugates contract researchers. Drawing on the data presented in earlier chapters, we make the case that the broader structures that organise the work of researchers require redefinition—both for the lives of contract researchers, and to sustain quality research.

What is work?

Together, these chapters build a logic for reform, rather than just a *wish list* of suggestions for both individuals and for institutions. Our argument is built on a number of key assumptions. First, we cannot begin to understand the extent of the problem without recognising the work and everyday lived realities of contract researchers. As Richardson and Heffernan (2019) suggest, in order to develop effective solutions, we need to know more about 'the competing demands of the job and what personal and work-related resources help to sustain healthy and committed academics' (unpaginated). We draw on Dorothy E. Smith's (2005, pp. 151–152) conception of work as:

> Anything done by people that takes time and effort, that they mean to do, that is done under definite conditions and with whatever means and tools, and that they may have to think about. It means much more than what is done on the job.

We have considered the many kinds of work contract researchers undertake, including work that is uncompensated and often invisible to the formal institution. Second, we understand these lived realities to be organised and shaped by wider institutional forces. That is, while we present individual stories, we show how the production of knowledge is subject to wider forces of advanced liberal rule that have triumphed since the 1980s.

The growth of contract research

Over a period of roughly four decades, the change in the research and academic institutional landscape in the US means that the traditional expectation to progress from a PhD to a tenure-track position no longer holds, and gaining tenure is now the exception (Institute of Medicine 2014). In many disciplines and countries, there is an oversupply of PhD holders compared to the number of academic jobs available (Crossouard et al. 2015; Institute of Medicine 2014). In countries such as Canada, the massification of PhDs (and associated oversupply of graduates) has been less pronounced (Crossouard et al. 2015). In Finland, the rate of employment for PhD holders is extremely high (97.6%) (Treuthardt & Nuutinen 2012), with around 80% of these being employed by universities or research institutions (Crossouard et al. 2015). However, the general trend globally has been a growth in the number of PhDs that outstrips the availability of academic jobs in universities (e.g. Gould 2015; Jaschik 2017; Larson et al. 2014). This change is largely driven by the inclusion of numbers of PhD students in performance metrics that incentivise universities to continue to increase numbers;

with no corresponding attempt to structure or regulate what happens to individuals wishing to pursue research careers after their PhD.

Outside of academia, higher degree research students can also face difficulty finding research work. As Boulos (2016, p. 93) states in an auto-ethnographic account of finding work in the UK after graduation: 'I quickly realized that holding a social sciences PhD was quite an obstacle to get into the job market'. While PhD graduates have advanced research skills, there may be a perception amongst employers that they lack professional work experience, particularly if they are 'inspired by the myth of the doctoral candidate in his/her ivory tower' (De Grande et al. 2014, p. 539).

Changes to government funding in many countries have also led to a decline in research positions in public agencies such as Australia's national federally funded science research agency, the Commonwealth Scientific and Industrial Research Organisation (CSIRO). The percentage of Gross Domestic Product the Australian government invested in research and development fell to just 0.56% in 2014—the lowest figure since 1979–80 (Howard 2015). Alongside decreased permanent job opportunities in government-funded research centres, changes to government funding have also had a significant impact on the nature of employment within universities. The increased reliance on *soft* money that comes from short-term funding (such as project specific grants) has made it riskier for universities to employ permanent research staff. Bourne (2018, p. 8647) explains that in the US, academic biomedical science research funding has been dramatically impacted by cuts to the National Institute of Health: 'Universities in the 1970s paid Principal Investigators [PIs] about 75% *hard* salary from their own coffers; those coffers in the twenty-first century pay PIs much less, forcing them to corral most salary as *soft* grant money'.

Another factor contributing to the unwillingness of universities to hire a permanent research workforce is the shift in related industrial conditions. For example, there has been a slowing down in the retirement of senior academics in the US after the mandatory retirement age was lifted in 1994. The slowing turnover of permanent academics has contributed to creating a far less certain career path, with a longer 'apprenticeship' for researchers hoping to secure tenure (Institute of Medicine 2014).

The Göttingen/Humboldt model of universities that saw teaching and research as dual university missions took hold across the nineteenth century and constituted *traditional* academic work as including both teaching and research. However, sweeping changes to higher education have shifted this balance. The massification of higher education (Tight 2019) has dramatically increased the number of students attending universities, which in turn has stretched academic workloads (Hill 2005). These changes have led to a reduction in secure *teaching and research* contracts, and a corresponding increase in academic staff employed on non-standard fixed-term and casual contracts in teaching-only and research-only roles (Allen-Collinson & Hockey 1998; Andrews et al. 2016). In Australian universities as of 2016, 85% of all university research-only positions were on fixed-term contracts; and fixed-term teaching-only staff conduct the majority of all teaching (Andrews et al. 2016). In the US, contingent faculty now comprise more than 75% of teaching staff nationally, and faculty contingency is now the norm (Cadambi 2016). In the Irish context too, there has been a reduction in permanent contracts and increased reliance on part-time, temporary staff for teaching and research roles (Courtois & O'Keefe 2015). The numbers of contract researchers in the UK has doubled since 2000 and increased more than tenfold over three decades (Universities UK 2010). Almost a decade on, 23% of all UK academic staff were employed as researchers on fixed-term contracts (in 2017/18) (HESA 2018).

In his book *Precariat: The New Dangerous Class*, Guy Standing (2011) has outlined a new theory of social class that includes the rise of a new group he calls *the precariat* (a portmanteau of precarious and proletariat). This group, he argues, can be thought of as *denizens*, or people who 'for one reason or another, have a more limited range of rights than citizens do' (23). As we will show throughout this book, many contract researchers contrast their limited rights with those of their tenured colleagues who have significant additional rights, entitlements and benefits. Standing (2011) argues that the precariat is not only defined by insecure income and working arrangements, but also by a 'lack of secure work-based identity' (16). As we will discuss in Chapter 2, there is evidence that rather than seeing contract research as a form of career-building, this form of work has a significant impact on academic and career identities. As one of our interviewees, Rachel, said when asked about her career path:

> Rachel: [Pause] Career path? [Pause].
> Interviewer: Mm-hmm.
> Rachel: [Laughter]. I don't believe I've ever had one of those!

Standing (2011, p. 16) describes that people in the precariat often accept jobs below expectation given their qualifications, leading to a sense of frustration or 'status discord'. Many researchers in our interviews talked about their inability to access work that required higher-level contributions (such as designing research), for which their doctoral studies had prepared them.

Who are contract researchers?

Contract academics are predominantly female and under 40, lending a gendered complexion to contract research (Bexley et al. 2013; Brown et al. 2017; McDonald 2015). The situation has not changed dramatically in the almost two decades since Hey (2001, p. 70) reported that the academy comprises a high proportion of men at the top of the hierarchy, with the majority of women working as 'a reserve force of contract researchers and temporary lecturers' or, as Eveline and Booth (2004) describe, in the 'ivory basement'. In Ireland, for example, it is estimated that 62% of precariously employed academics (both teaching and research) are women, earn less than €10,000 annually, and continue in insecure work for approximately eight and a half years post-PhD; and that 70% of permanent academic positions are held by men (Ivancheva 2015, pp. 41–42). Many of the women in this 'reserve force' have children, which creates further disadvantages in terms of career progression—a phenomenon increasingly being recognised as a 'motherhood penalty' (Maxwell et al. 2019; Weeden et al. 2016). The gendered nature of this work divide led Oakley (1995) to describe precariously employed academics a 'lumpen proletariat' who were expected to perform the 'housework' of the academy (p. 22). These workforce demographics have created significant interest in casualisation of the academic precariat from feminist scholars (e.g. Angervall et al. 2015; Bosanquet et al. 2017; Thornton 2013). There is also growing recognition that a wide set of institutional and cultural factors have contributed to the gendered nature of precarious work in higher education (*cf* Murgia & Poggio 2018).

There has also been a steady increase in the age at which people start PhDs, noted in the US (Institute of Medicine 2014) and the UK, with the number of starters on full-time doctoral courses aged 21 and under dropping by 45% over the period from 1996–97 to 2004–05 (Higher Education Funding Council for England 2009). Currently 48% of those people commencing PhDs are 28 years or older (Universities UK 2009). The age of PhD commencement raises an additional set of challenges in terms of how research work intersects with attendant demands of different life stages, particularly when understood in light of the lengthy (if not indefinite) apprenticeship phase of the research career.

Although our interest for this book is in precariously employed researchers, their contractual status must be positioned in the context of broader changes to employment in higher education, including the explosion of short-term teaching-only employment (often known as adjunct faculty in the US; or sessional lecturers in Canada and Australia). Terminology used in the US refers to staff with continuing or permanent employment contracts as having *tenure*; with a precursor to achieving tenure being for staff to be accepted into a *tenure-track* post, i.e. one in which it is possible to progress towards tenure (in contrast to positions in which tenure is not an option for career progression). Discussion of non-tenured researchers in policy reports also generally positions them as *early career researchers*, typified by statements such as that short-term funding 'provid[es] bridging funding to retain early-career researchers beyond the scope of funding for a specific project' (Universities UK 2009). However, situating insecurely employed researchers as *early career* implies that being a contract researcher is a temporary state of affairs, and that individuals are expected to transition to permanent contracts within a defined period of time. As the majority of researchers we talked to indicate, this is no longer the case due to the dwindling number of tenure-track and permanent research positions.

We have mapped some commonly used titles to indicate the interplay between research-only, teaching-only and teaching and research positions (by level of insecurity) (*see* Table 1.1)

There has been a significant growth in both short-term research-only and teaching-only positions. For example, in Australia, full-time equivalent (FTE) research staff increased by 121% between 2001 and 2013, and teaching only staff grew by 66%, in comparison with a mere 17% growth in teaching-and-research staff (Andrews et al. 2016, p. 10). Yet, even these figures are misleading. The use of categories such as FTE (rather than actual headcounts) in university reporting make it all but impossible to understand how many employees work on insecure and part-time research contracts (Connell 2019). Indeed the UK's University and Colleges Union has criticised the failure to collect adequate data about hourly paid academic staff as cynically motivated obfuscation of the true situation (UCU 2019). The range of terminology and configurations used, as shown in the table above, can also frustrate discussions of contract research because of the different labels used for academic roles and types of contract, many of which overlap. Many of the reports on higher education and research conflate academic roles, or do not clearly define their use of terminology, failing to

Table 1.1 Configurations of research and teaching employment

	Research only	Teaching only	Teaching and research
Security/length of employment	Common titles	Common titles	Common titles
	Research Assistant, Research Associate, Research Fellow, Contingent Faculty, Postdoctoral Fellow	Adjunct, Sessional (tutor or lecturer)	Lecturer, Senior Lecturer, Assistant Professor, Associate Professor, Professor
	Basis of employment	Basis of employment	Basis of employment
Very short-term	Very short-term casual or short-term contract (e.g. 0–100 hours to complete a very specific task such as a literature review, data analysis or editing)	Very short-term casual or short-term contract (e.g. casual contracts for a tutorial, guest lecture or specified hours of marking)	Combination of contracts from the *research-only* and *teach-only* strands of employment

	Short-term (e.g. 3–12 months) to complete a range of tasks on a particular project	Short-term (e.g. during term) teaching contracts	
	Fixed-term (e.g. a contract that spans the funded life of a project. This would typically commence after funding has been achieved)	Fixed-term (e.g. full year teaching contracts)	
Permanent	Tenured research-only positions	Tenured teach-only positions	Tenured academic positions that combine teaching and research. Many of these are based on a ratio (e.g. teaching: 40%; research: 40%; and service: 20%)

distinguish contract researchers from permanent teaching and research staff, or treating precarious employment as a problem composed only of sessional and short-term teaching. These reports can obscure contract researchers as a category of staff requiring policy attention in their own right.

Policy context

In the UK, policy on research careers is produced under the auspices of Universities UK. However, much of the policy related to researchers and research careers is over ten years old and the pace of change in industrial conditions means much of it fails to capture the current realities of work for insecure researchers. For example, England has seen changes such as the abolition of student grants in favour of student loans and tuition fees; a tethering of research funding to measurement frameworks; and the introduction of increased student numbers as a policy objective (DfES 2003). These and other policy-led changes have wrought profound consequences for the nature of universities' role, function and employment practices. This is not to say governments and institutions have not made attempts to understand and rectify harmful policy effects on precarious workers in Europe and internationally. In Australia, for example, the Australian Research Council (2018) released a *Research Workforce Statement* that aims to better understand different career trajectories (such as considering the needs of researchers who have taken career breaks).

In the UK, the *Concordat to Support the Career Development of Researchers* (UKRI 2008) provides a comprehensive discussion of researchers and research careers, proposing a set of seven principles for the good management of researchers and their career development. The *Concordat* was intended for implementation in all UK institutions that employ researchers and was subject to an independent review (UKRI 2018, p. 4) that stated 'most progress is required in the support of early career researchers in academia. An increased understanding is needed of the UK researcher community through better data gathering and in the tracking of researcher careers'. The subsequent *Concordat Consultation Report* (Concordat Strategy Group 2019) concluded that the lack of data about contract researchers created difficulty in evaluating progress against stated principles.

The *Concordat* is treated, and referenced, by other UK research and researcher-related policy as satisfying the policy requirement around contract researchers. However, as the experiences of researchers in later chapters indicate, it is yet to have made a substantial difference to experiences of insecurely employed researchers in the UK. The forthcoming update of the Concordat is intended to have more 'teeth' and sets out more explicit obligations for institutions, acknowledging its variable impact to date (Concordat Strategy Group 2019).

The Australian and UK experiences are indicative of wider policy trends in other Westernised nations where little attention has been paid to contract research. Gaughan and Bozeman (2018) describe the US situation as one characterised by 'coalitions of powerful higher education stakeholders, a weak federal government, [and] controversial overlapping policy domains' (358). These conditions inhibit the development of coherent agendas and interest groups across domains and regions through which to influence policy. We believe that the growth of contract research means this significant stakeholder group must find ways of collectivising so as to actively participant in policy research, development and enactment.

Feeling the effects of managerialism

We have already touched on a number of macro level trends that have seen an expansion of uncertain career paths and insecure employment. Sitting behind these trends are broader global policy shifts, including the trend in Westernised higher education institutions towards managerialism. Research institutions (including universities) now adopt business values and approaches to employees and their management. The target-driven regulation of university services (teaching and research) places the emphasis on quantifiable knowledge-related outputs, rather than knowledge processes. Enterprising universities in contemporary times focus on research that will earn them prestige in the global education market, which typically helps to generate greater income from student fees and research grants. Both tenured and non-tenured staff are expected to meet universal indicators of quality such as publication in high-quality journals (Mingers & Willmott 2013). Managerialist approaches have contributed to the rise of inequity within academia, by further privileging those in a position to meet these ever-shifting criteria, such as tenured academics at elite universities. The corporate turn has turned researchers from scholars in their own right to 'disposable resources' (Nadolny et al. 2011).

The increased use of temporary contracts to employ academic staff in advanced liberal democracies is a conscious choice on the part of organisations as they seek to reduce costs associated with employing people (Brady & Briody 2016). Continuing contracts are seen as particularly risky by university management because they are harder to manage given the increasing reliance on soft money (through government and philanthropic grants), and because they come with generous entitlements, redundancy provisions and other complex industrial protections (Andrews et al. 2016). It is anticipated that a worsening funding landscape (e.g. in the UK and US) will accelerate this process, despite the already low rate of successful grant applications (Andrews et al. 2016; Brady & Briody 2016). In this context, temporary contracts mitigate against uncertainty about the production of research by managing the supply of, and demand for, staff (Brady & Briody 2016).

For employers, the identification of 'good performance' and 'talent' among contract research staff takes time because of the nature of research. Research indicators such as demonstrating 'real world' impact or achieving publication in esteemed journals can take years (Brady 2017). The use of fixed-term appointments enables institutions to dispense with the costs and responsibilities of managing tenured employees and avoid or delay what is seen as a risky and irreversible decision to offer tenured contracts (Brady & Briody 2016). Managerial practices have transferred risks from employers to employees, and afforded institutions the ability to maintain an image of prestige while managing uncertainty about human resource needs (Brady & Briody 2016).

Increasing casualisation within higher education mirrors employment trends in other sectors (e.g. Friedman 2014; Mensitieri 2012; Trades Union Congress 2014). The European Commission reports that 'The possibility of finding a permanent job decreased slightly between 2002 and 2017, as the share of temporary employees in the EU increased from 11% in 2002 to 13 % in 2017' (Eurostat 2018, p. 1). The use of temporary contracts, however, is particularly prevalent in the academic sector, with no other sector in the UK having such a large proportion of temporary staff in its workforce (Bryson & Blackwell 2006). Temporary researchers are not merely covering for permanent staff who are absent or not yet recruited—they are a deliberate part of human resources strategy (Brady & Briody 2016). Although short-term employment mitigates human resources risks, this strategy also carries negative consequences for both institutions and individuals.

Consequences for researchers

As long ago as 1994, the UK *Association of University Teachers* report (Bryson & Tulle-Winton 1994) observed a range of career and employment disadvantages experienced by contract researchers. They concluded there was little evidence of the existence of a career structure or career development; that contract researchers were reported to be exploited in terms of hours worked, their roles and responsibilities, and recognition granted and that they experienced dissatisfaction due to insecurity, low pay, low status, isolation and inequality of opportunity (Bryson & Tulle-Winton 1994; Sukhnandan 1997). Contract researchers continue to report high levels of job-related disadvantage, such as persistent financial insecurity and inadequate remuneration (Brown et al. 2010; Courtois & O'Keefe 2015; University and College Union 2019). It is unsurprising then that the UK Research and Innovation (UKRI) (an independent organisation commissioned by the UK government to foster research) also raised concerns about the subjectivities these conditions produce among researchers, noting 'there are groups of researchers, such as those who have had multiple, short-term contracts and/or long service through fixed-term contracts, who do not feel integrated within the institution, and report less positive feelings about their employer, job and career' (UKRI 2009, p. 14).

Fixed-term contract researchers as an academic precariat have become a reserve army of workers with ever shorter, lower paid, hyper-flexible contracts and ever more temporally fragmented and geographically displaced hyper-mobile lives (Ivancheva 2015). Under such conditions, while many fixed-term academic staff seek a continuing academic appointment, most are pessimistic about the prospects of achieving this goal (e.g. Andrews et al. 2016).

The nature of fixed-term research affects prospects for advancement in terms of tangible and intangible benefits and opportunities, including access to internal funding, and opportunities to gain important and valued skills (such as grant writing) that are typically required for achieving tenure and promotion (Andrews et al. 2016; Broadbent et al. 2013). The timescales and institutional policies related to temporary contracts may restrict or prevent staff from undertaking certain activities that would support career advancement and promotion prospects, such as supervising PhD students and bidding for research money (Brady & Briody 2016). As such, contract employment can deny fixed-term researchers access to many of the employment conditions and opportunities that govern their long-term success as researchers (e.g. Hooley et al. 2010). Paradoxically, this kind of work can restrict their ability to compete for permanent positions, when they are competing with others who have had these opportunities (Harney et al. 2014).

28 *Situating the contract research career*

Given the problematic nature of contract research for individuals, there is widespread aversion to having multiple successive temporary contracts for those whose main objective is a permanent position (Brady & Briody 2016). Post-PhD, many researchers are grateful to acquire temporary contracts and the opportunity to build experience and produce publications. In this way, contract research can serve as a 'pseudo-probationary period' for a permanent academic role (Brady & Briody 2016). Their experiences, however, can exacerbate divisions between tenured and non-tenured academic staff (Brady & Briody 2016). Fixed-term contracts can be perceived as divisive (Broadbent & Strachan 2016; Eveline & Booth 2004) and experienced as an entrenched class divide within institutions between temporary and tenured staff (Brown et al. 2010). In symbolic terms, the divide between temporary and permanent academic staff positions tenured work as the 'core' and pushes temporary roles to the periphery (Kimber 2003). Within this two-tier workforce the tenured core experience relatively good employment conditions and security while those on the periphery are subject to poor conditions and insecurity. There are limited opportunities for contract researchers to move from the periphery to the core (Broadbent et al. 2013) and few exit points out of precarious work within academia (Courtois & O'Keefe 2015).

Their relatively lower status marginalises contract researchers and deprives them of a voice in the workplace, in which speaking up is treated as class subordination (Brown et al. 2010). Precarious workers on whose labour the university relies on to function are often rendered invisible (Courtois & O'Keefe 2015). Some contract researchers report experiencing this invisibility as disconnection from their permanent academic colleagues (Brady & Briody 2016). While many of the interviews presented in this book illustrate these tensions, there are also examples of organisations working to buck these trends. These examples, discussed further in Chapter 4, demonstrate that the divisive practices that position contract researchers as *Other* in the academy can be overcome—at least to some extent—in localised settings.

A final word

Given the changes described above, we might wonder why doctoral graduates (including ourselves) pursue academic careers. For those who do, there may be a tension between having stimulating work set in a context of poor management and an absence of career paths (Nadolny & Ryan 2015). In spite of feeling that their work is meaningful, many contract researchers have considered leaving their universities due to their uncertain, insecure and poor working conditions (Siekkinen et al. 2017). In the case of scientific research in the US, this has resulted in an accelerated pace of researchers leaving academia such that the time it takes for half of a doctoral cohort to exit the field 'has shortened from 35 years in the 1960s to only 5 years in the 2010s' (Milojević et al. 2018, p. 12616).

The impact of casualisation on teaching and learning has been documented (e.g. University and College Union 2019), but the impact of casualisation on *research* has received less attention. Given the pressure on institutions to demonstrate research success and impact, it is in the interest of universities to retain talented researchers (Universities UK 2009). Institutions risk losing talented staff if they leave to seek more secure employment elsewhere (Brady & Briody 2016) and those able to do so are likely to be researchers with greater capital. This contrasts with the more positive conceptualisation of contract research as a 'boundaryless career', offering flexibility to both researchers and the institution (Harney et al. 2014).

We conclude this chapter with an extract from Simon's blog post on *Patter* (https://patthomson.net/) because we still believe that research careers can be fulfilling, and 'worth the fight':

> As I said at the beginning of this post, career contracting was not exactly what I thought I was signing up for when I decided upon a career in academia. Among many other aspirations, what I really wanted to do was write. With time and persistence I have found a position that affords me more opportunities to write than the majority of my colleagues, wherever they stand on the ladder. In this sense I think career contracting can be worth the fight.

Note

1 In the US, contingent faculty refers to full-time non-tenure track, part-time and graduate student employees. This figure refers to both teaching and research positions.

References

Allen-Collinson, J. & Hockey, J., 1998, 'Capturing contracts: Informal activity among contract researchers', *British Journal of Sociology of Education*, vol. 19, no. 4, pp. 497–515.

Andrews, S., Bare, L., Bentley, P., Goedegebuure, L., Pugsley, C. & Rance, B., 2016, *Contingent Academic Employment in Australian*

Universities, Melbourne: LH Martin Institute and the Australian Higher Education Industrial Association, www.lhmartininstitute.edu.au/documents/publications/2016-contingent-academic-employment-in-australian-universities-updatedapr16.pdf, accessed 7 March 2018.

Angervall, P., Beach, D. & Gustafsson, J., 2015, 'The unacknowledged value of female academic labour power for male research careers', *Higher Education Research & Development*, vol. 34, no. 5, pp. 815–827.

Australian Research Council (ARC), 2018, *Research Workforce Statement*, www.arc.gov.au/sites/default/files/strategy_research_workforce_statement_2018.pdf, accessed 30 August 2019.

Back, L., 2016, *Academic Diary: Or Why Higher Education Still Matters*, Cambridge: MIT Press.

Ball, S.J., 2015, 'Subjectivity as a site of struggle: Refusing neoliberalism?', *British Journal of Sociology of Education*, vol. 37, no. 8, doi: 10.1080/01425692.2015.1044072.

Barcan, R., 2013, *Academic Life and Labour in the New University: Hope and Other Choices*, London, UK: Routledge.

Bexley, E., Arkoudis, S. & James, R., 2013, 'The motivations, values and future plans of Australian academics', *Higher Education*, vol. 65, no. 3, pp. 385–400, doi: 10. 1007/s10734-012-9550-3.

Bosanquet, A., Mailey, A., Matthews, K.E. & Lodge, J.M., 2017, 'Redefining "early career" in academia: A collective narrative approach', *Higher Education Research & Development*, vol. 36, no. 5, pp. 890–902, doi: 10. 1080/07294360.2016.1263934.

Boulos, A., 2016, 'The labour market relevance of PhDs: An issue for academic research and policy-makers', *Studies in Higher Education*, vol. 41, no. 5, pp. 901–913.

Bourne, H.R., 2018, 'Expansion fever and soft money plague the biomedical research enterprise', *National Academy of Sciences*, vol. 115, no. 35, pp. 8647–8651.

Brady, M. (2017). 'Temporary employment contracts in academia: a real option view', *Tertiary Education and Management*, vol. 23, no. 2, pp.153–169.

Brady, M. & Briody, A., 2016, 'Strategic use of temporary employment contracts as real options', *Journal of General Management*, vol. 42, no. 2, pp. 31–56, doi: 10.1177/030630701704200204.

Broadbent, K. & Strachan, G., 2016, '"It's difficult to forecast your longer term career milestone": Career development and insecure employment for research academics in Australian universities", *Labour & Industry: A Journal of the Social and Economic Relations of Work*, vol. 26, no. 4, pp. 251–265, doi: 10.1080/10301763.2016.1243438.

Broadbent, K., Troup, C. & Strachan, G., 2013, 'Research staff in Australian universities: Is there a career path?', *Labour & Industry: A Journal of the Social and Economic Relations of Work*, vol. 23, no. 3, pp. 276–295, doi: 10.1080/10301763.2013.839082.

Brown, T., Goodman, J. & Yasukawa, K., 2010, 'Academic casualization in Australia: Class divisions in the university', *Journal of Industrial Relations*, vol. 52, no. 2, pp. 169–182, doi: 10.1177/0022185609359443.

Brown, J., Shaw, E., Pickup, R. & Morbey, H., 2017, *Contract Researcher Audit and Survey–Foundation Report January 2017*, University of Lancaster: Faculty of Health & Medicine, Lancaster University, https://eprints.lancs.ac.uk/id/eprint/84449/1/FHM_Contract_Researcher_Audit_and_Survey_Foundation_Report.pdf, accessed 25 August 2019.

Bryson, C. & Blackwell, R., 2006, 'Managing temporary workers in higher education: Still at the margin', *Personnel Review*, vol. 35, no. 2, pp. 207–224.

Bryson, C. & Tulle-Winton, E., 1994, *A Survey of Contract Research Staff in UK Universities*, London, UK: Association of University Teachers.

Cadambi, D.M., 2016, 'Contingent faculty of the world unite! Organizing to resist the corporatization of higher education', *New Labor Forum*, vol. 25, no. 1, pp. 44–51, doi: 10.1177/1095796015620408.

Concordat Strategy Group, 2019, *Consultation on the Recommendations of the Independent Review of the Concordat to Support the Career Development of Researchers*, www.vitae.ac.uk/policy/concordat-to-support-the-career-development-of-researchers/concordat-consultation-report-april19.pdf, accessed 20 June 2019.

Connell, R., 2019, *The Good University*, Clayton: Monash University Publishing.

Courtois, A. & O'Keefe, T., 2015, 'Precarity in the ivory cage: Neoliberalism and casualisation of work in the Irish higher education sector', *Journal for Critical Education Policy Studies*, vol. 13, no. 1, pp. 43–66.

Crossouard, B., Andres, L., Bengtsen, S.S., Castano, L. P.G., Keefer, F.M. & Pyhalto, K., 2015, 'Drivers and interpretations of doctoral education today: National comparisons', *Frontline Learning Research*, vol. 3, no. 3, pp. 5–22.

De Grande, H., De Boyser, K., Vandevelde, K. & Van Rossem, R., 2014, 'From academia to industry: Are doctorate holders ready?', *Journal of the Knowledge Economy*, vol. 5, no. 3, pp. 538–561.

Department for Education and Skills (DfES), 2003, *The Future of Higher Education Government White Paper*, London, UK: The Stationery Office.

European University Institute, 2019, *Academic Careers Observatory: USA Academic Career Structure*, USA: European University Institute, www.eui.eu/ProgrammesAndFellowships/AcademicCareersObservatory/AcademicCareersbyCountry/, accessed 7 March 2018.

Eurostat, 2018, *Temporary and Part-Time Jobs on the Rise*, https://ec.europa.eu/eurostat/web/products-eurostat-news/-/WDN-20180813-1, accessed 30 August 2019.

Eveline, J. & Booth, M., 2004, '"Don't write about it" Writing 'the other' for the ivory basement', *Journal of Organizational Change Management*, vol. 17, no. 3, pp. 243–255.

Flaherty, C., 2018, *A Non-Tenure-Track Profession*, www.insidehighered.com/news/2018/10/12/about-three-quarters-all-faculty-positions-are-tenure-track-according-new-aaup, accessed 30 August 2019.

Floersch, J., Longhofer, J.L., Kranke, D. & Townsend, L., 2010, 'Integrating thematic, grounded theory and narrative analysis: A case study of adolescent psychotropic treatment', *Qualitative Social Work*, vol. 9, no. 3, pp. 407–425.

Friedman, G., 2014, 'Workers without employers: Shadow corporations and the rise of the gig economy', *Review of Keynesian Economics*, vol. 2, no. 2, pp. 171–188.

Gaughan, M. & Bozeman, B., 2018, 'Institutionalized inequity in the USA: The case of postdoctoral researchers', *Science and Public Policy*, vol. 46, no. 3, pp. 358–368, doi: 10.1093/scipol/scy063.

Georghiou, L., 2015, *Value of Research Policy Paper by the Research, Innovation, and Science Policy Experts (RISE)*, Brussels, BE: European Commission, https://manchester2016.esof.eu/files/_pdf/georghiou-value_research.pdf, accessed 4 July 2019.

Gould, J., 2015, 'How to build a better PhD', *Nature News*, vol. 528, no. 7580, pp. 22–25.

Harney, B., Monks, K., Alexopoulos, A., Buckley, F. & Hogan, T., 2014, 'University research scientists as knowledge workers: Contract status and employment opportunities', *International Journal of Human Resource Management*, vol. 25, no. 16, pp. 2219–2233, doi: 10.1080/09585192. 2011.561241.

HESA, 2018, *Higher Education Student Statistics: UK, 2016/17 – Qualifications Achieved*, www.hesa.ac.uk/news/11-01-2018/sfr247-higher-education-student-statistics/qualifications, accessed 17 May 2019.

Hey, V., 2001, 'The construction of academic time: Sub/contracting academic labour in research', *Journal of Education Policy*, vol. 16, no. 1, pp. 67–84, doi: 10.1080/02680930010009831.

Higher Education Funding Council for England, 2009, *PhD Study Trends and Profiles, 1996–97 to 2004–05*, https://webarchive.nationalarchives.gov.uk/:HECFE, accessed 7 March 2018.

Hill, D., 2005, 'Globalisation and its educational discontents: Neoliberalisation and its impacts on education workers' rights, pay and conditions', *International Studies in Sociology of Education*, vol. 15, no. 3, pp. 257–288.

Hooley, T., Kent, R., Williams, S., Hale, C., Oliver, L. & Thompson, J., 2010, Hard times? Building and sustaining research capacity in UK universities issues in research management and administration, *Vitae*, vitae.ac.uk, accessed 17 May 2019.

Howard, B., 2015, 'Pursuing other professions: PhD supply and demand', *Chemistry in Australia*, pp. 26–29.

Institute of Medicine, 2014, *The Arc of the Academic Research Career: Issues and Implications for U.S. Science and Engineering Leadership: Summary of a Workshop*, Washington, DC: The National Academies Press, doi: 10. 17226/18627, accessed 17 May 2019.

Ivancheva, M.P., 2015, 'The age of precarity and the new challenges to the academic profession', *Studia Europaea*, vol. 60, no. 1, pp. 39–47.

Jaschik, S., 2017, 'The shrinking humanities job market', *Inside Higher Education*, www.insidehighered.com/news/2017/08/28/more-humanities-phds-are-awarded-job-openings-are-disappearing, accessed 17 May 2019.

Kimber, M., 2003, 'The tenured 'core' and the tenuous 'periphery': The casualisation of academic work in Australian universities', *Journal of Higher Education Policy and Management*, vol. 25, no. 1, pp. 41–50.

Larson, R.C., Ghaffarzadegan, N. & Xue, Y., 2014, 'Too many PhD graduates or too few academic job openings: The basic reproductive number R0 in academia', *Systems Research and Behavioral Science*, vol. 31, no. 6, pp. 745–750.

Macfarlane, B., 2010, 'The morphing of academic practice: Unbundling and the rise of the para-academic', *Higher Education Quarterly*, vol. 65, no. 1, pp. 59–73.

Maxwell, N., Connolly, L. & Ní Laoire, C., 2019, 'Informality, emotion and gendered career paths: The hidden toll of maternity leave on female academics and researchers', *Gender, Work & Organization*, vol. 26, no. 2, pp. 140–157.

McDonald, T., 2015, 'Insecure work in unis is gendered', *Agenda*, NTEU, www.nteu.org.au/women/article/Insecure-work-in-unis-is-gendered-%28Agenda-2015%29-17939, accessed 30 August 2019.

Mensitieri, G., 2012, *The Most Beautiful Job in the World*, Paris: La Découverte.

Milojević, S., Radicchi, F. & Walsh, J.P., 2018, 'Changing demographics of scientific careers: The rise of the temporary workforce', *Proceedings of the National Academy of Sciences*, vol. 115, no. 50, pp. 12616–12623.

Mingers, J. & Willmott, H., 2013, 'Taylorizing business school research: On the 'one best way' performative effects of journal ranking lists', *Human Relations*, vol. 66, no. 8, pp. 1051–1073.

Murgia, A. & Poggio, B. (eds), 2018, *Gender and Precarious Research Careers: A Comparative Analysis*, New York: Routledge.

Nadolny, A., McNeil, K., Ryan, S., Groen, B. & Bhattacharyya, A., 2011, '"McJobs": A comparison of the academic and McDonald's casual worker experience', in *The Way Forward—Austerity or Stimulus?' 13th Path to Full Employment Conference and 18th National Conference on Unemployment*, pp. 131–140, https://nova.newcastle.edu.au/vital/access/services/Download/uon:25248/ATTACHMENT02?view=true, accessed 7 March 2018.

Nadolny, A. & Ryan, S., 2015, 'McUniversities revisited: A comparison of university and McDonald's casual employee experiences in Australia', *Studies in Higher Education*, vol. 40, no. 1, pp. 142–157.

Nikolaidis, E. & Maroudas, L., 2013, 'Institutional changes and the expansion of flexible forms of employment in higher education: The case of Greek universities', *Journal for Critical Education Policy Studies (JCEPS)*, vol. 11, no. 3, pp. 127–145.

Oakley, A., 1995, 'Public visions, private matters', in *Professorial Inaugural Lecture*, London: Institute of Education, University of London.

Petrova, M., 2017, 'On academic job insecurity and the ultimate tenure: Thoughts on contract. Thoughts from contract no. 17', *Naturejobs Blog*, http://blogs.nature.com/naturejobs/2017/03/22/on-academic-job-insecurity-and-the-ultimate-tenure/, accessed 4 July 2019.

Rea, J., 2015, 'Organizing against the widening gap in academic job security in Australia', *Academic Matters*, https://academicmatters.ca/organizing-against-the-widening-gap-in-academic-job-security-in-australia/, accessed 25 August 2019.

Richardson, P. & Heffernan, A., 2019, 'Our university workforce has become a fragmented, casualised 'gig economy', The problems we face', *AARE EduResearch Matters: A Voice for Australian Educational Researchers*, www.aare.edu.au/blog/?p=4087, accessed 4 July 2019.

Siekkinen, T., Kuoppala, K., Pekkola, E. & Välimaa, J., 2017, 'Reciprocal commitment in academic careers? Finnish implications and international trends', *European Journal of Higher Education*, vol. 7, no. 2, pp. 120–135, doi: 10.1080/21568235.2016.1248990.

Smith, D.E., 2005, *Institutional Ethnography. A Sociology for People*, Lanham: Altamira Press.

Standing, G., 2011, *The Precariat—The New Dangerous Class*, London: Bloomsbury.

Sukhnandan, L., 1997, 'Indispensable but under-valued: The exploitation of contract research staff', *Teaching in Higher Education*, vol. 2, no. 3, pp. 333–339, doi: 10.1080/1356215970020312.

Thornton, M., 2013, 'The mirage of merit: Reconstituting the "ideal academic"', *Australian Feminist Studies*, vol. 28, no. 76, pp. 127–143.

Tight, M., 2019, 'Mass higher education and massification', *Higher Education Policy*, vol. 32, no. 1, pp. 93–108.

Trades Union Congress, 2014, *Casualisation and Low Pay: A Report for the TUC*, London: TUC.

Treuthardt, L. & Nuutinen, A., 2012, *The State of Scientific Research in Finland 2012. Publications of Academy of Finland 7/2012*, www.aka.fi/en-GB/A/Decisions-and-impacts/The-state-of-scientific-research-in-Finland/Previous-reviews/The-state-of-scientific-research-in-Finland-2012/, accessed 8 June 2019.

UK Research and Innovation (UKRI), 2008, *Concordat to Support the Career Development of Researchers*, www.vitae.ac.uk/policy/vitae-concordat-vitae-2011.pdf, accessed 7 March 2018.

UK Research and Innovation (UKRI), 2009, *Sustainability of the Research Workforce*, www.ukri.org/files/legacy/skills/sustainability-oftheukresearchworkforce-pdf/, accessed 6 January 2019.

UK Research and Innovation (UKRI), 2018, *Review of the Concordat to Support the Career Development of Researchers*. www.ukri.org/files/skills/concordatreviewreport-jun2018-pdf/, accessed 8 June 2019.

University and College Union, 2019, *Stamp Out Casual Contracts*, www.ucu.org.uk/stampout, accessed 30 August 2019.

Universities UK, 2009, *Securing World Class Research in UK Universities: Exploring the Impact of Block Grant Funding*, www.universitiesuk.ac.uk/policy-and-analysis/reports/Documents/2009/securing-world-class-research-in-uk-universities.pdf, accessed 8 June 2019.

Universities UK, 2010, *The Future of Research*, www.universitiesuk.ac.uk/policy-and-analysis/reports/Documents/2010/the-future-of-research.pdf, accessed 8 June 2019.

Weeden, K.A., Cha, Y. & Bucca, M., 2016, 'Long work hours, part-time work, and trends in the gender gap in pay, the motherhood wage penalty, and the fatherhood wage premium', *RSF: The Russell Sage Foundation Journal of the Social Sciences*, vol. 2, no. 4, pp. 71–102.

2 Becoming and being a contract researcher

The multiplicity of *making it*

I recently spent a year working for three different institutions, teaching and supervising MA students. These posts were all temporary and part-time, and my job title and salary was different in each place even though my role was essentially the same. The universities were in different parts of the country, so I spent a lot of time and money on train travel. Luckily, I had friends I could stay with, so I didn't have to pay for accommodation too.

Aside from the precariousness and low status of such posts, the downsides mainly related to academia's systems not being set up for people with multiple jobs. As a temporary staff member, I didn't have an office to work from, so had to meet my students in whichever windowless storeroom happened to be free. Computer software I use every day got very confused when I tried to access different institutional accounts on the same device. And there were minor irks like forms for submitting proposals or applying for jobs generally allowing for only one current institution despite the fact that having several part-time jobs is now commonplace for recent PhD graduates.

Admin systems, supervision procedures, the allocation and management of project roles, the work I undertook, and how my work was evaluated all varied across the three institutions, but this actually yielded insights into best (and worst) practice. Despite the lack of job security, I enjoyed significant autonomy, and something I only really appreciated with hindsight was that, as a temporary and 'remote' staff member, I didn't have to get involved in staff meetings, periodic course reviews and all the other administrative baggage that comes with academic work.

—Reflections of a contract researcher

Entry into contract research

The most common way to enter a contract research career is via higher degree research studies. While some people actively seek an academic or research career, others describe having fallen into research work during their undergraduate or postgraduate research degrees, particularly doctoral studies. Take Chris, for example, who describes:

> I never planned to do research as a career, I never planned to do anything with my PhD other than put it in a little pile and then move on and go into teaching for the rest of my life. So I was working as a teacher, I had a part-time—three

Becoming and being a contract researcher 39

> days a week—role which suited me perfectly, and then my PhD supervisor—I'd done some marking and stuff for him, nothing really very onerous—rang me up and said "Oh, we haven't got anyone else, do you think you could do some qual [qualitative] analysis on about five interviews on a project?" And I went "Oh, yeah, that's fine. Yep, bit of extra money, that's fine".

This informal, piecemeal offering was the beginning of Chris' research career, which isn't unusual. Many researchers said small contracts often snowballed, led to further contracts, and ultimately, a career. Of course, there are many whose decision to move into research work is more intentional. These researchers typically commence work under the guidance of their honours, Master's or PhD supervisors, and have a career plan in which casual research and teaching is viewed as a stepping stone towards a traditional academic position.

Experienced researchers suggest that if you are hoping to move into this space, developing this experience as early as possible in your degree is important. Rachel said:

> if there are particular areas that you're interested in, maybe even to just reach out to some of these people working in the area, and go "Hey, I've just graduated, or I'm graduating from such and such and really interested in this area, and being an research assistant", you know? I started out doing stuff like data entry and reference lists.

A number of the researchers we interviewed had taken the initiative to contact academics they either knew or were aware of through their own research interests. Amy said:

> The very first [university research] job that I got was by cold calling, knocking on doors of researchers and saying, "I love your research, here's my CV". And I was lucky enough to get called the next day with work. And then everything else has just spread from that.
>
> Interviewer: So 11 years of word of mouth?
> Amy: 11 years of word of mouth, absolutely.

This focus on cold calling and word-of-mouth does not mean casual, fixed-term and tenured academic jobs are not advertised. Pitt and Mewburn's (2016, p. 93) analysis of academic job advertisements in the Australian state of Victoria found many positions:

> were predominantly research-focussed and on short- or fixed-term contracts. [W]e suspected that many of these early career academics are being employed to undertake the research, or at a minimum, the data analysis, on pre-existing research programmes that might be "written up" by others after the incumbent's contract ended.

While many contract positions are not formally advertised, securing advertised fixed-term positions is typically a highly competitive process that might involve working on research that has already been conceptualised or even commenced. Challenges associated with this type of work are discussed in Chapter 3.

Being offered work while completing a PhD or Master's is not the only entry into research work. Some researchers establish relationships with lecturers during their undergraduate studies and are subsequently offered work with a view to taking on post-graduate research down the track. Some researchers undertake short-term administrative contracts that eventually enable them to move into a research stream without undertaking doctoral studies. Jill's experience (see Vignette 2.1) provides an illustrative example of how this happens.

Vignette 2.1: Jill's experience of moving from administration to research

Jill had run her own business for a number of years. In 2010, with her children at school, Jill decided that working for someone else would provide her with a steadier income. Jill did not have a post-graduate qualification and began to look for a general/administrative role. Her undergraduate studies and work history were primarily in international education and marketing. Jill responded to an advertised position in a research institute and was employed as an administrative assistant. However, she soon realised she was undertaking similar work to research assistants on the project:

> Well, I was really put on to do admin, but then ... We would have research assistants then that would do the surveys and data entry and analysis and then write up reports, but then he started not

> employing those ... [so] I was doing it ... [Eventually] I said "can't you change the role to research?"

Despite her employer deciding not to change her job title, Jill started to use the title *research project officer* on her CV, along with a description of the kinds of tasks she undertook in the research institute. Jill has gone on to work at a number of universities, cooperative research centres and research institutes. She is increasingly aware of the need for a PhD to continue to be successful in finding work but, as she is nearing retirement, Jill doesn't see this as a viable option for sustaining her contract research career:

> the problem I'm in now is a lot of the research jobs ... a lot of them will want you to have a PhD or working towards, it or have an undergraduate degree in that field, whereas mine is completely different ... Mine is a business communications degree ... I can write; I can take complex issues and put them into plain English to communicate ... [but I don't have a PhD].

Jill's experience can be contrasted with the fortunes of many PhD graduates aspiring to research careers who decide instead to take on university administrative work in the hope of getting their 'foot in the door', as Helen Sword commented:

we get a lot of ... people who are local who are doing a PhD for whatever reason, and don't want to leave, so then they're looking for jobs afterwards, what can you do with the PhD? There are a lot of jobs in the university that are not, they're not really post docs, they're more administrative positions, but maybe working in the research office, administrating grants, or working for the vice chancellors office researching policy at other universities or, you know, those sorts of things, and it's very striking to me how many people with PhDs end up in those jobs, and I doubt a single one of those people intended to, but it does give them a kind of stability, and yet they're always looking for something else ...

It is important for those embarking on a research career, intentionally or otherwise, to develop an understanding of the nature of research employment and make employment decisions in the context of what they are hoping to achieve.

Progressing as a contract researcher

The changing nature of employment means academic career paths can no longer be assumed to take the form of a series of sequential moves from PhD to tenure before an eventual promotion to the professoriate. Instead, progress for the majority of precariously employed researchers involves navigating a context in which some entrepreneurialism is required to move away from the 'post-doctoral treadmill' (Edwards et al. 2011).

Developing the academic identity

Developing an academic identity is critical, particularly for those who work on projects that do not fit their own expertise and interests. Building your own identity as a researcher can be a difficult process, involving deep consideration of why you have embarked on this path and the type of work you want to do. Thomson and Kamler (2013, p. 16) describe that 'the narrativised self is not a neutral account' because it is shaped by cultures, the perceptions of others as well as how we see ourselves. Emma, who had just moved into a non-academic position after almost a decade of trying to obtain tenured work was asked what advice she would give to someone about to embark on a research career. Mourning her own move out of academic work, she said:

> Look, I think that people who are reaching the end of the PhD, the people who are going to do this—you can't stop them ... because they want to do it. It takes a couple of years for the pain to get really painful. So, they ... it's not that they think they are going to get a job. If they are sensible, they will know. [They will have] already have worked that out. It's that they *want* to keep writing. They *want* to keep doing the research that they are doing. They have a vocation ...

The scholarly identity is often 'rooted in our perceptions of how others view scholars' (Thomson & Kamler 2013, p. 17). As such, views around research as a vocation or passion sustain beliefs that working for free is part of what it takes to be a *real* academic.

Discourses of passion for academic work have been described as part of an 'idealised past—the Golden Age of academia' (Cannizzo 2018, p. 91). Coin's (2018, p. 302) research describes the experiences of Italian casual academics, making links to feminist histories of domestic labour:

> women's domestic labour was presented as an act of love, a natural attribute of the female personality that required no monetary compensation. Today, academic labour is often presented as a labour of love. Young, female academics' scholarly labour is treated as a form of self-expression that fulfils an affective need, hence turning the actual conditions of labour into afterthoughts.

This *labour of love* was often accompanied by an understanding that despite their best efforts, tenured work may never materialise. Allan (2019) has described this reality as the rise of 'hope labour', which has emerged in precarious job markets. This work draws on a logic of investment (i.e. being prepared to work for free in the hope of future employment) in the hope of a return on investment. Gregg (2017, p. 48) describes a situation in which, 'low compensation for a high workload ... [is] rationalised as a feature of the job'. Sam, for instance, talked about 'governing ourselves in order to fit into [university] hierarchies ... In order to keep our toehold in institutions, for very good reasons—we love doing the research'.

This pervasive view of academic labour is entwined with complex power relations between contract researchers and employing academics. Perceptions of unfair treatment by supervising academics can be a recurring reality, but one frequently accepted as part of being a contract researcher. As Jill said:

> a lot of the time you have to deal with other academics. But you really do need to have a thick skin. And you have to come up with ... I mean for some of the comments that are made you feel like you are that small [pinches her fingers together to indicate a tiny amount]. And you're worthless or something ... Just the way that [academics] would talk to [casual researchers]. That they didn't do a good enough job, or they would make a comment like, "I wouldn't talk to that person" ... "and they haven't done a good job".

Many of the researchers we talked to felt their subjectivities were impacted by both their insecure employment conditions and the way they were positioned at work in relation to their tenured colleagues. Issues such as not having a desk or space to work, not being invited to meetings or included in email lists meant contract researchers often felt alienated and de-legitimised. Some described bullying behaviour that they felt could not be challenged without risking future work.

Disempowering aspects of research work left many resenting their working conditions and their ability to develop an academic identity in line with their research passions, while accepting that being a contract researcher means learning to live with uncertainty. Reflecting on her sense of what it means to be a contract researcher, Laura referred to notes she had compiled before she arrived at her interview. She said:

> I've just written here, "We know that each one of us are replaceable and there's not a single thing important about us", I think is the general view ... I've seen about six people just disappear, no mention that they were leaving or that their contract wasn't being renewed. This is just at this place alone, this is my third year there ... They just don't get renewed ... And then all of a sudden there's new person and you go, "Oh hello, I don't think I've met you", and they go "Oh yeah I'm the new such and such", and you go "What? Where's ..."

This 'ontological insecurity' (Giddens 1991) in which researchers' economic and intellectual identities were impacted by the lack of continuity and order had a profound impact on almost all of the researchers we talked with.

Feelings of shame and loss were common as continuity and the ability to make a substantial, ongoing contribution—to the academy, to their research field, to their families—were lamented. Numerous researchers we talked with made comments such as 'what's wrong with me?' or 'is my work not valued?' For Giddens (1991), while the ontologically insecure are grappling with the lack of continuity, the ontologically secure are probably oblivious to these kinds of existential questions. While both tenured and contract academics face significant challenges in neoliberal times, contract researchers experience substantially less security or autonomy in pursuing their research interests. There is a clear expectation for tenured academics to establish an ongoing and cohesive program of research. Contract researchers, on the other hand, may view their position as *research-for-hire* and expend substantial time, energy and emotion on looking for work, managing their lives around potential work and delving into new research areas as the work dictates. The sense of imposter syndrome (Clance & Imes 1978) can be heightened for contract researchers, whose attempts to navigate this intellectually and emotionally challenging landscape may never lead to secure employment.

Bourdieu (1988, p. 76) wrote of the 'unjustifiable privilege' of academic work; however, these privileges are not available to all who work in research. University hierarchies operate through prestige and power relations that are 'obtained and maintained by holding a position enabling domination of other positions and their holders' (Bourdieu 1988, p. 84). The issues of power and privilege align with Mensitieri's (2012) research exposing the, often abysmal, working conditions of precarious workers in the French fashion industry. In a sector valorised as prestigious and glamorous, workers are frequently underpaid, or not paid at all, leaving many unable to make ends meet in order to work in this prestigious industry. As she describes:

> The message is, you don't have to be paid because you are lucky to be there at all. Working in fashion is hyper socially validating, even if you're unpaid. That's an important point for me. Fashion presents itself as something exceptional, a world outside the ordinary.
> (quoted in Marsh 2018, p. 10)

Passion for work within the *ivory tower* of research can similarly override the deep uncertainties contract researchers hold about their academic identities. The vast majority of contract researchers have invested heavily to secure a career trajectory, and have a deep commitment to the intellectual project, despite their insecure employment conditions. As Graeme states in his interview:

> How badly do you want to be an academic? I think it takes the fun out of it. That combination of overwork and insecurity makes it hard to still feel ... to still get that good feeling that you get ... from research and stuff, and *that's* what might have got you here in the first place.

Being strategic and developing your research story

Reflecting on their career paths, the researchers we talked with agreed that adopting a strategic approach to building a career was essential. A strategic approach requires consideration of what is important to you and talking to others about possible strategies for moving into work aligned with your career goals. Researchers talked about considering their research *niche* and ensuring that, as far as possible, taking work that supported them to build a narrative around this niche, by developing expertise on a specific topic, or in a specific set of methodologies and/or theories.

Setting your own goals and identifying future research priorities where work might be available is an important long-term strategy. Intentionally observing the progression strategies of peers and established academics is helpful for understanding how they have established and maintained their careers. Rachel said that early in her career she made a conscious decision to 'get as much different experience as I could ... mainly in quantitative research, purely because that was just something I found that was in demand'. Rachel has been working on casual contracts across a number of universities, research institutions and hospital research centres for more than a decade post-PhD. Despite her vast experience, she acknowledged the importance of making a connection between disparate jobs:

> if you can find or see a connection between the different things you do. Like for what I do—they're in really different areas—but if someone said what's your expertise, or what are you? I'd say a methodologist; and I've worked in areas A and B.

Maintaining employment as a contract researcher therefore requires the ability to build a narrative around one (or more) research interests; and the ability to demonstrate you have acquired the skills, disposition and track record that academics looking for research support will need. Contract researchers typically have multiple areas of focus for their career planning: fulfilling the needs of their current employer; obtaining the skills needed to secure contracts in the immediate future; and, developing a cohesive track record with long-term employment prospects in mind.

Having a sense of your research interests and goals and being able to articulate your area of expertise enables you to confidently explain your work to others (including potential employers). Dedicating time to constructing an area of expertise also enables you to seek out professional activities and networks that will move your career in a direction that aligns with your own research interests. Reflecting on a long career as a researcher, Cochran-Smith (2012, p. 101) suggests that working on research you care about will ultimately sustain your passion and stresses the importance of understanding your own research identity:

> One of the most important lessons I learned as an emerging scholar was that I needed to figure out how to position myself and where to locate myself in terms of research ... Many people have used the metaphor of "conversation" to refer to broad groupings of research questions, methods, agendas, and areas of focus within even broader general fields.

While some institutions have structures in place that assist researchers in building a research profile, it is important that you take time to develop a cohesive narrative around your work. Inger Mewburn (2017) the creator of the popular *Thesis Whisperer* website was encouraged by a family member to write her own 'mission statement' to help develop her research interests and personal brand. Being able to articulate the variety of work undertaken over months or years in this way takes attention and skill. Penny, a researcher from New Zealand said:

> ... just trying to seek connections between the things that you do [is important], because I've been asked [by potential employers] questions like "Where do you see yourself in five years?" ... Um, retired! [Laughter] ... not really ... I think employers, people like to see, and meet people that have goals ... [so] just try and see the links between all the different things that you've done.

To draw on Bröckling's (2015, p. 20) notions of the 'entrepreneurial self', contract researchers must become 'entrepreneurs of their own lives'. An illustrative example of one researcher who took this approach over many years is provided below in Vignette 2.2

> ### Vignette 2.2: Amy's experience of finding a common thread in a 'patchwork of contracts'
>
> Amy has been employed in various research capacities (both in the private sector and universities). Early in her career she worked for philanthropic organisations doing work, including grant writing. When her family relocated, she decided to find local academics whose work aligned with her own interests in social justice for vulnerable populations. She cold-called a number of academics seeking possibilities for work. These conversations led her to short-term university tutoring, where she met other university academics. Amy later gained a PhD scholarship and casual research work at the same university. In reflecting on this period in her career, she said:
>
>> I think ... when I used to watch friends who were building their academic career and I was watching them from the comfort of my own little PhD experience and not having to worry ... I had a scholarship so I didn't have to worry as much about getting contracts. I was thinking, "If I ever go into contract research I'm

> going to really strategically align myself with the people that I really want to work with and I'm going to make sure that everything makes sense in terms of my own professional goals and I want it to add value to my own professional path".

Amy's strategy for finding and selecting work was careful and considered. As a sought-after casual researcher, Amy took into account factors such as whether or not the role fit within a narrative she wanted to create about her career, and whether the colleagues she would work for shared similar ethics, values and research interests:

> I actually have to take a breath and think about each of my contracts career path-wise. I guess—like anything—you pick and choose what you learn from each experience. I have one contract right now where I'm learning so much about leadership, about generous leadership. I have another contract where it's the subject matter that I'm the most interested in. I took the contract thinking it would lead to some teaching and it turns out it's not. That's been really disappointing thinking, "Why did I do this if it's not going to lead me somewhere?"
>
> I guess it is what you make of it and what you choose to learn from each experience. So of course there's something you can draw from and I suppose

> these things will look good on my CV even though [it's] ... a CV with a patchwork of contracts ... What does that look like? How do you put that together?
>
> ... I think, I suppose it comes down to formulating a story. I think of the way that academic CV kind of templates look and they don't fit the story of the contract researcher. So it may just be up to me or to us to kind of re-envisage that ... what a CV should look like and kind of tell the story ... because someone who's just looking at it for ten minutes through a pile of other CVs, they may not see the threads.

Near the end of her PhD, Amy was beginning to worry if her intentionality would pay off. The reality of constructing a CV that included her 'patchwork of contracts' with a common research thread was challenging. At the time, she began to question whether this approach would lead to permanent employment:

> In some ways I do feel as though I've done that and I have said no to things that I didn't think really fit within the scope of what I'm trying to do with my career or my interests and passions. But it isn't easy because you do get almost to the point of desperation or just worrying so much about that stability, so that first issue that you think, well I should just take anything that comes along because

> you don't know when something else is
> going to come along, and you can't hold
> out hope.
>
> Some months after Amy made these remarks, she
> was offered a position in a new university. Despite
> not having any existing contacts at the new university, Amy obtained the role through a competitive process due to the skill set she had acquired,
> and because she had built a narrative around her
> research passion that aligned with her new role.

Building a publication track record

Working towards a long-term research career inevitably means understanding how research work is assessed and valued. Tenured academic staff are generally measured (with respect to their research work) by their ability to attract research funding, and to publish in highly ranked journals (Gruber 2014). Your publication record will be a critical factor in successfully securing employment and research grants. Hence, one of the most common pieces of advice for PhD students and non-tenured researchers is to develop a 'high-quality' publication record. It is valuable for researchers to understand how the quality and impact of their publications will be judged, both through citations and ratings of journal quality. For example, Journal Citation Reports in Web of Science and SCImago Journal Rank, are commonly used measures of journal prestige; while Altmetrics measures social media references to scholarly material. Publishing in high-quality journals, or with high-quality publishers, and being able to demonstrate the impact of your work, through citations, invitations for presentations and acknowledgement by external agencies has become increasingly important for all researchers.

Despite these expectations, there is frequently a disparity between how work is allocated to contract researchers, and how their long-term employability is judged. Contract researchers often spend time on project management, reading, data collection and analysis, with little paid time made available for writing. As we describe further in Chapter 3, working on other people's projects can feel piecemeal, and might not provide you with opportunities to build a strong publication record. It is typical for contract work to include specific research tasks such as reviewing literature, collecting and analysing data; while writing and publication are often not offered to contract researchers. As Heather described it:

> But certainly, my mentor is telling me I need to get some papers done, or else I won't be considered at the end of the one-year contract basically … It's something I want to do anyway but it was always at the bottom of the pile … I just didn't have time to do much else. I know I need to do it and keen to do it, and it's nice to be able to have time to do it …

Regardless of work demands or a lack of paid opportunities to publish, the reality is quality publications are essential in the current *publish-or-perish* environment (Ivancheva 2015). As such, many contract researchers develop a publication plan for themselves with specific goals to produce publications in their 'own' time, unpaid and generally outside of the projects on which they are working. When asked about his personal publication plan, Sam said:

> There is [the publication plan I created for myself] but ... no, if I'm really thinking about it ... it's more external ... pressure. So I guess just if I'm thinking of ... basically when [the university is] going around sacking people ... In the two institutions I've been at, they look at your public ... they're assessing people on "how much are they publishing? How active are they?" And that sort of thing. And so, no, I would say it's a kind of "in-university [pressure]". I'm more conscious of what the university thinks of me.

Sam's comments reflect Alvesson and Spicer's (2016, p. 40) notion that many casual academics have an 'awareness of the need to construct a kind of idealised "entrepreneurial academic self" for the purposes of securing employment or research grants'. However, we contend researchers also engage in this work because they have a passion for research, a desire to contribute to their field and because they see publication of their work as an important part of their academic identity. Bourdieu (1988) described reading and writing as the pleasures of academic life; a privilege of the position. However, for contract researchers, this 'pleasure' is not always part of the position. Instead, this work frequently occurs outside of paid employment, in your own time, in order to build visibility and employability.

Acquiring in-demand skills

While building a strong narrative of research interests is an ideal, the nature of contract employment means researchers cannot always work on projects that align with their own expertise or interests. Working on new projects can be a challenge, that may require you invest time and energy into acquiring new disciplinary knowledge, learn new literature and methodological approaches, and develop other new skills (such as the use of new technology). Vanessa summed up this issue, stating: 'picking up a new ball and running with it is time consuming'. The effort required to build new areas of expertise can be intensified by the lack of targeted professional development for those on short-term or casual contracts. As Laura said:

> So professional development is one of the things that I feel, I just can't get. Because projects are always externally funded or even if it comes from within the organisation, every aspect of that funding is very carefully allocated, and because you're never considered core business to the institution, even if you've been there nine years.

Nadolny and Ryan (2015) point out that even McDonald's—an organisation often derided (e.g. Ritzer 1993) for its Tayloristic approaches to work—provides casual staff with clear, paid training opportunities. Many researchers spend time outside of paid employment developing new skills (Brown et al. 2010). Standing (2011) has described the ongoing need for training as a feature of the precariat workforce as researchers often need to train on their own time, simply to ensure ongoing employability. Rightly or wrongly, the responsibility for ongoing skill development often falls to individuals, highlighting the importance of adopting a strategic and proactive approach towards learning. Rachel said:

> ... a lot of places have access to Lynda.com which is free online courses, they have courses in a lot of different data programs, skills, so it might even be worth just watching some of those—because they're free—and just trying to learn, if you have time.

Rachel, who has worked on contract for well over a decade in various settings, said this approach had been the key to her ability to securing ongoing work.

When it is available, financial support to attend professional development will often come from a specific project budget, which means it will need to support the researcher to meet the needs of the research. If training is not related to an ongoing project with an available budget, then it will likely be much harder to access financial support. It is rarely, if ever, the case that contract researchers will have access to faculty funding, or the research allowances and accounts tenured academics can build.

Restricted access to formal development and training is only one of the challenges in developing in-demand skills. Experience such as grant-writing and research budget management is most often developed on-the-job. This may require you to be proactive and strategic in looking for opportunities to acquire experience. While this work (for example, offering to write grants) can lead to new contracts, it does not guarantee an invitation to join future research. Kate described having been employed to carry out significant research and writing for a nationally competitive grant application. When the grant application was successful, however, the tight budget meant that she ultimately only 'got two days' work out of that grant. Two days!'

Even if you take steps to be proactive, the nature of academic work means it may be challenging to access these opportunities. Amy talked about her attempts to gain important skills in grant-writing, and her attempts to develop a successful grant that might lead to further employment:

> I've taken steps, I've researched grants, grant funding programs and approached people who I thought I had similar research interests and I've gone to them and said, "Should we think about writing a proposal for this grant? Maybe creating a small project". Trying to carve out work for myself, build work for myself. And they're supportive and they say, "Oh yeah, that'd be great. I don't have any time right now, let's do it next year … And I think, well that's great. They didn't say no but between now and next year I need work and preferably work that I'm passionate about and that I have some expertise in and that I can richly contribute to and not just plan meetings and do administrative duties.

Nevertheless, working closely with others is a vital part of academic work, and can provide the basis for a satisfying and ongoing research career, which is discussed in Chapter 3.

Managing quality research

The experience of working on larger projects affords contract researchers the chance to understand how research projects are designed and managed, and can provide insight into the pressures of research work. Many contract researchers we talked to expressed dismay at

Becoming and being a contract researcher 61

the limited time academics had available to devote to research tasks. The lack of lead researchers'[1] time to dedicate to projects can be a source of tension and raise ethical questions around how quality research is produced. The reality is, working on collaborative research is very different to doctoral research where significant time can be devoted to tasks such as reading and analysis. Kathy said:

> I think that we underestimate the importance of the literature ... and I sometimes wonder where I have seen somebody ... sort of just lightly repurpose a lit review that I've given to them and then put it into their work, I've thought to myself, "My God, you didn't even read it! You know, I did this thing and I sent you a body of literature, and you didn't read it!" ... You just trusted that my peripheral reading of things to sort of cobble together the parts, because I assumed that then you were going to do your homework with it ...

The issue of contract researchers being called on to complete tasks quickly with little time to discuss the research work in detail with academics is extremely common. Limited opportunities for communication and collaboration can result in miscommunication with tenured academics and can create further concerns around research quality. Danielle, for example, said she had been disappointed with her early contract research work and, as a result, had 'learned through that process to ask lots and lots of questions' to better understand the expectations of her research supervisors and to try to engage them more deeply in the process of understanding the literature and analysis. Many researchers expressed considerable dismay at what they saw as sub-standard research practice due to the time pressures of tenured teaching and research academics.

The hidden work of a contract researcher

> People who have jobs have no idea how hard people that don't have jobs work ... you can't understand unless you live it.
> —Laura

We now turn to consider the many forms of work that are invisible to the institution. Jobs such as filling in timesheets, completing administrative requirements, finding new contracts, managing the complex 'work-life collision' (Pocock 2003) that can occur when employed without industrial entitlements such as holiday or sick leave, consume time and energy. We have spoken to researchers who have worked through caring responsibilities, illness and even chemotherapy in order to sustain their income and to avoid jeopardising their opportunity to secure new contract work. Laura described:

> It's everything from HR and finance systems through to how decisions are made, through to professional development, through to all these things that are ... are only given to staff that are full-time really. Except that you *work* full-time ... but you're not *considered* a full-time staff member.

There is a significant burden on the precariat to manage their employment in ways that do not impact permanent employees. This work is rarely made visible, acknowledged or supported. To understand the depth of this issue, it is worth returning to Nadolny and Ryan's (2015) comparison of casual work at McDonald's and universities. Their research highlights how McDonald's, with its focus on efficiency, has developed seamless, simple, online processes, for example, to pay staff; in contrast, casual academics describe this work as complex, laborious and slow. Where McDonald's has invested heavily into managing its highly casualised workforce, universities have not. Amy describes the challenges of managing multiple contracts that fall into different industrial categories—despite the similarities of her work:

> It's so complex—and the fact that [even] within the same faculty … things are done a bit differently and sessional contracts are so different from casual contracts, which is different from professional contracts. And I've got all three of those. It does bend the mind a bit.

She went on to explain:

> Some of the difficulty as well was that lecturers are so busy, and keeping up with the contracts of their research assistants is understandably far down on the priority list. So I had one contract finish and there was quite a gap until the next one started but I was working between those times so trying to finagle that into a timesheet and it felt strange because I was having to basically make up the days.

This issue of facing complex administrative requirements just to be paid came up a number of times, with researchers talking about the inadequacy of systems to cope with the nature of non-tenured employment. We heard multiple stories of starting work and not being paid until weeks or months later as a result of institutional processes. Again, we contrast this with permanent staff (everyone from permanent cleaners to senior leaders) who not only access additional entitlements, but whose pay is deposited automatically. Laura:

> I had someone from HR ring me once and say, "You know there's a problem with what you're doing with your timesheets, you have to follow correct organisational processes", and I said, "Okay fair enough, what have I missed?" And it came down to fact that I worked for one person across multiple projects, right? So within a day, you might do two hours on one project, one hour on another. But as a casual you're not allowed to be employed for less than three hours. So on a timesheet, they have it set up so that a timesheet exists per cost code. So in a day I might write one hour for that day for that project—when in fact I was employed for the entire day. And so I said this and she said, "Well that's not right", and I said, "Yes it is right", "Well you know, it can't be in the system like that", and I said, "So you're asking me to actually lie and allocate the day to a different day?", and she said, "No, no it's very important, it's part of our audit that staff are honest with their timesheets".

> I have been honest with my timesheets! It's that the system doesn't let me say "here was a day in which I was employed", I sat in the same chair!

This inability of university systems to take account of the lived realities of these employment structures creates significant work for researchers. An important lesson is to keep track of the time you spend on work, which leads on to the next issue raised by researchers—the importance of charging fairly for the hours you work. The *hidden work* of being on contract is extensive and has substantial impact on the lives of researchers beyond their employment. José's experiences (see Vignette 2.3), for example, highlight the significant additional pressures faced by the most vulnerable researchers (such as those with visa requirements).

Vignette 2.3: José's experiences of Contract (and Immigrant) Research

Holding a Tier 2 visa while working as an RA presented several difficulties. A major problem has to do with the difference in timetables between the availability of new positions and my visa requirements. It is quite normal for researchers on contract work to worry about their end of contract and the need for finding new employment. It is also understandable that positions are not always available and, arguably, it might be reasonable to expect that upon the end of a contract one will have to endure a short spell of unemployment before securing the next job. As an academic aware of his precariat situation, I took extra measures to save a portion of my income each month for the possibility of finding myself out of contract work (perhaps I should also add that I am not entitled for unemployment benefits). This would have been fine if I were a resident able to remain in the country while out of work. I might have been able to use my savings to carry me over to the next contract, but this is not a possibility. Under Tier 2 visa requirements, I am forced to leave the country within two weeks of the date of employment termination. The possibility of staying in England to secure another job becomes very slim and any window between one contract and a new one carries the threat of removal. This adds considerable stress, because finding a new position to replace an ending project carries additional criteria—the new job needs to be, more or less, starting exactly when the current one ends (or before). A job opening that begins, say, a month after the end of one contract job becomes problematic and perhaps irrelevant.

This problem is not only in regards external positions. Even in situations where a favourable line manager wishes I would stay in post by 'finding money' from other projects—something rather prevalent in the sector—this does not necessarily mean I could stay. Work visas are tied to a particular employer and a particular position. What would amount to a simple HR task of switching positions can easily become a failure to meet my visa conditions or a cause for issuing a new visa tied to the 'new' position. Thus, even within a supportive and understanding environment, where senior managers are happy with my work and even have funding to 'top-up' their previous budget commitments for my retention the process is out of their hands.

To this I should also add the financial burden of issuing these visas. Each new contract, having to be tied to a new visa, also requires new visa fees to be paid. At a UK university, the university paid visa fees (currently at £700), but not for the mandatory NHS Surcharge of £200 per year that I had to bear (even though I pay income tax like everyone else). Other universities in the sector do not follow this policy and the visa fees are also paid by researchers. Thus, a contract for two years, as an example, would cost £1,100 to issue a visa for. And in case the researcher wants to move to a new position within this timeframe, a new application needs to be made with the amount payable again, regardless of what was issued previously. Although the Home Office states that money will be refunded for periods of double-pay, I have yet to receive any refunds.

Lastly, there's also room to comment about the so-called Hostile Environment. The news [is] filled with horror stories about the removal of highly skilled workers due to Home Office incompetence and, at times, against the law. The atmosphere is one of lack of trust in what the Home Office promises and a feeling that even if one meets all requirements, something will pop up as a problem. This means that visa applications are very stressful and even after securing a position there is a fear that the visa application will be turned down due to change in requirements or a misunderstanding with the officials.

Charging fairly for your work

In 2006, Baranay (2013) wrote of her conversations with casual researchers that 'the greatest consistency was in their claim that they worked far more hours than they were paid for' (p. 41). While the 'ideal' academic has increasingly been positioned as someone who works much more than a standard 9-to-5 job (Sang et al. 2015), contract researchers do not have access to the same privileges and benefits of their tenured colleagues, so it is questionable whether they should be subject to these same conditions. (Whether these conditions are fair for any academic staff is also up for discussion).

A problem for contract researchers centres around the nature of any academic work: it is often difficult to estimate how long intellectual work might take. Take writing as an example. To quote Helen Sword (2017), academic writing is a creative process that requires *air and light and time and space*. The unpredictable nature of this work often raises ethical dilemmas for the contract researcher: If you are being paid to contribute to a publication as part of a research team, how many hours should you spend on this creative work? If you submit timesheets, how many hours might you charge for? What about time spent reading literature? Should you include time spent submitting timesheets? These (and many others) were all questions that contract researchers we talked to had asked themselves as they wondered what constituted fair compensation for their time.

The nature of intellectual work is that it is time consuming and does not necessarily produce outcomes quickly. The process of reading for research requires substantial commitment of time and expertise but has received relatively little attention as part of the research process

(Harney et al. 2014; Ivancheva 2015). The effort required to develop knowledge of existing literature within a new field is not to be underestimated. All researchers are required to read extensively to familiarise themselves with the field and its discourses. Once familiar with seminal literature, researchers need to stay abreast of current developments in the field and read for their writing, all of which can be a challenge. However, when you are paid to work with unfamiliar disciplinary knowledge, methodologies and theoretical approaches, it could be argued that the challenge of academic reading is even greater. Despite the volume of literature that you may need to engage with (often very quickly), research contracts often do not include dedicated reading time. It is more common for contracts to include tasks such as managing and conducting data collection, analysing data and assembling results. Time for building deep understandings of how research fits within the field can be limited. *Imposter syndrome* loomed in discussions with researchers, who were often concerned they weren't reading or writing 'fast enough'.

Assembling research reports and publications requires 'a good deal of hard work that never makes it onto the page' (Hayot 2014, p. 116). This means much of the work of contract researchers may never be visible as an output. Many researchers reported being unsure of how much of this background work of reading in the field can be counted towards their work in terms of paid hours. Searching for and reading papers for a literature review can mean wading through many articles that aren't relevant (enough) to the topic at hand. Amelia said:

> I used to think, "[What I have produced] isn't so much, [for] the five hours. I better do ten

> hours". And that totally is more of a problem because then they expect ten hours' worth, which is not possible in five hours.
>
> And look, you know what? I would have that conversation [with other contract researchers] on a daily basis. If I go and make a cup of coffee, do I need to stop the clock? You ... know? It was all the time. I would start as soon as I dropped the kids to the bus stop ... plus, you know, as I'd say be putting in [timesheets to be paid for] maybe four hours and you're like, "But I've sat here for seven hours today".
>
> And ... you skim through really quickly and try to accumulate enough as it looks like a reasonable amount ... It's not quality.

The amount of time you feel you can justify on tasks such as reading may be different depending on the length of your contract. For example, a multi-year contract may include reading and writing time; but if you are only employed for a few months, a few weeks, or even a set number of hours this may not be the case. Tensions over what counts as work are exacerbated where researchers feel their performance requires the production of tangible outputs rather than less visible contributions to the research. As Danielle indicates, she believes her performance as a researcher is judged on the end results of her work, including meeting deadlines for writing:

> when I produce pieces of writing, like literature reviews, and when I can be organised and timely, and meet the deadlines that I said I'd meet, those are all indications that I'm doing good work, I hope.

The vast majority of researchers we spoke with reported they routinely underreported the number of hours they worked, claiming only for the time they have spent producing physical evidence of their work. The invisible work of research, like reading, was often unclaimed in a bid to appear more productive. To draw on Ball's (2000) work, the focus may become oriented towards producing 'fabrications' or tangible evidence of work. Depending on your circumstances, it may be possible for you to talk with your employers about what is expected, particularly when you are working in an unfamiliar research area. You might be able to negotiate some dedicated reading time even if it includes the need to produce tangible evidence such as a reference library, an annotated bibliography or literature review.

The increasing project management approach that dominates universities in contemporary times means that academic work has been intensified, with researchers (both contract and tenured) expected to do more in less time (e.g. Nikolaidis & Maroudas 2013). These moves have very immediate effects on contract researchers. For example, Laura said:

> [In my second year on one project I was changed from full-time to] only a 0.8 [of a full-time load] position. So I had to do [the same amount of work] in four days, even though the year before it was a five-day position. So I was like right okay, I had that extra day in which I knew I was going to need to set up something to carry into this year, so I'd put the word out at my current work place and I was then allocated to three projects for that one day. And I remember saying, "Okay that's one day,

that's three projects", and it was very, very clearly pointed out to me that, in fact, it was my responsibility to demonstrate my ability to manage a workload.

In Chapter 4, we consider some possible responses for researchers (and their tenured allies) in these kinds of scenarios. However, we also suggest you make yourself aware of your rights by familiarising yourself with institutional and industrial policies. We contend that a paradigm shift is needed in which researchers are paid for the hours they work, rather than it being an expectation that many more hours are worked for each hour of pay.

Finding the next contract

An additional form of work for non-tenured researchers is finding work. Actively looking for work, often through your current work is vitally important to ensuring continuity of employment. Ashley said:

> ... this sort of work not only required me to act like someone who's self-employed in an administrative way, but I had to kind of learn to sell myself and advertise. You almost have to advertise. And you have to think about every single thing I'm doing is advertisement for your next job or your next ... you want ... so much of it is word of mouth...

Ashley is not only referring to formally approaching potential employers, but rather, the attention required to the reality that all work might be seen as a reflection of your identity. This desire to look efficient—perhaps, as the academic 'superhero'—often sat behind the decision not to charge for all work undertaken. Decisions around which skill you hone, which contracts you take, who you work with and so on are all important. David said:

> I think the biggest challenge, and it applies to this one too, is finding continuing employment. That's always the overarching thing in the back of your mind. And it's important because it takes away from the time you have to do other things. So if you spend a lot of time applying for jobs, that's time out of doing potentially your roles, it's time out of your personal or family recharge time, aside from work. So it impacts how you're balancing your time and how you're managing your time quite a bit.

As we will discuss in Chapter 3, an important avenue for reducing stress and finding ongoing work is through your relationships with other contract researchers, and with ethical tenured colleagues.

Managing periods of under or unemployment

Unfortunately, managing periods of under or unemployment is part of the hidden labour for many contract researchers. Even when employed and working in excess of a standard full-time workload, researchers typically invested time in looking for future work opportunities so that when one contract expired, they could quickly commence a new job. They also spent time organising their lives (and finances) around possible periods of under- or un-employment. Laura, for example, explained that this had been the reason it had taken her a week or two to respond to the invitation to participate in this project:

> That was part of the delay in getting back to you. I was actually just putting all my time into trying to set up the next thing. Because I'm currently doing four projects and I get great feedback from whoever I work for—I'm not worried about that. It's the extra time that you've got to put in to in terms of going, okay "What's around?", "When would that be?", "They want me to start now? Damn it, I'm already doing a full-time load", but I'm going to need that [later on].

Balancing the timing of contracts is a recurring issue, and one that requires both luck and hard work, as both José (Vignette 2.3) and Laura's situations indicate. Contracts rarely line up seamlessly, so researchers must often make decisions that take into account their financial and career goals and interests. As Penny said:

> ... [I ran into a professor who I worked for a few years ago]. She said a comment the other day. "You should have stayed with us". Something like that. [But] I can't stay where there's no work! I would have loved to stay there.

Penny described that the professor had hoped she would stay on and be available when more work became available on the professor's project, but that long periods of unemployment were simply not viable financially. Penny had teaching contracts at a number of universities to fill in the gaps between research contracts—one of the so-called 'freeway flyers' (Lynch-Biniek 2017) who commutes long distances between universities to deliver teaching. However, this created a new problem for Penny who soon realised her new teaching commitments meant she was no longer available for research contracts when they became available. Penny had also learned that offers of work from professors she had worked with over the years were often delayed, or ended up being relatively short term due to the nature of funding academic work:

> I'm supposed to start work in a little while with—supposedly—some other researchers ... but again, they're little ones [short-term contracts] ... and I haven't heard from them ... They're so busy with everything else. And there is no way I can do the field work travel [to regional and remote towns], so that's again working around teaching.

The paradoxical situation of having to turn down desirable work because of existing commitments to less favourable work was particularly disheartening. Many researchers we talked to discussed working in other areas, including retail jobs, because they were easier to balance with contract research and provided continuity of income. The project-basis of research created dilemmas for contract researchers; for example, should you accept work with a supervisor you know is difficult to work with when you have an employment gap? Should you take on a contract that takes you away from your discipline when you are waiting for another project to materialise?

Structural disadvantages can also be created by the timing of contracts. For example, lead researchers such as principal investigators or chief investigators and universities often align contracts with their own holiday or leave plans. For people on contracts of less than 12 months, this often meant no pay at important times such as over the Christmas/New Year season or during long breaks in teaching. Laura, who had worked in multiple settings recounted her time in a religious-based institution:

> They have as part of their creed social justice, right? [sarcastic tone] And that must be why they make sure the contract stops before Christmas. Right in the middle of December, and then all of a sudden you get re-employed again on the 12th January. I raised it with them, and just said [sarcastic tone], "It's really strange how all of these contracts just seem to miss Christmas. It's amazing".

However, having worked on contract for many years, Laura had learned to be as proactive as she could, for example, by arguing for changes in how she takes any leave entitlements:

> Because in every single contract I have, it's written in that I have to take my leave before the end of the contact ... and for every single time, I send a letter to HR saying "I am a contract employee, when this contract ends, that's it". So actually, I need my leave approved so

> that it can be paid to me, because there will be a period of time when I will be looking for work. Or to cover any gaps between the next project is starting. Even if it's already teed up.

Although Ashley knew that, in many instances, a lack of work was the product of structural realities (such as the end of a funded project), there was still a sense that:

> ... one part of your head goes "Yeah okay I know that my university is really tight, and I know that there's no money" but then the other voice goes "but maybe they'd find it if they really wanted to keep you?" I think that aspect is harsh and it's quite stressful, like when you're coming up to the next contract date and you're like "I don't know what's going to happen next?"

These kinds of comments further illustrate how precarity has a significant impact on the academic identity. Even when employed, the anxiety around finding the next job can present an ongoing challenge, as Blair said:

> ... it takes away from your kind of direction of thinking—it's a distraction. You can't throw yourself completely into the project in front of you because you've got to have your eye on what's next.

Sadly, this can have long-term personal costs; for example, one of our participants talked about having decided against having children because they were not sure they could afford it.

Health, ageing and contract research

If you or anyone in your family have complex health care needs, this can have a significant impact on your experiences working as a contract researcher. While many contract researchers reported that they felt pressure to be able to move between universities to secure work, moving away from central locations can be difficult for those requiring specialist health care. Others reported that they were concerned that their health issues, or those of family members, would be viewed negatively and would impact negatively on their opportunities for future work. In this instance, the importance of working with ethical and caring supervisors becomes increasingly important (see Chapter 3). Rachel talked about the stress she experienced after a major surgery saying that despite having some sick leave, her key concern while in hospital was getting back to work:

> Like, other people's jobs, if they are full-time, they get things like stress-leave, or six months maternity leave, and all of that sort of thing. We just don't get that.

Managing the cost of chronic healthcare for ongoing conditions is a significant consideration, and sometimes makes it challenging to meet contract requirements. Laura:

> I did try to explain to my supervisor, "Sorry, at the moment I'm trialling all this different medication, all that means is that it ... Mornings are more difficult, so if I'm in the office, I would appreciate some flexibility to

come in at, say, 9 o'clock or 9:30. I can work later". You know? And I think it was … Sort of response was, like, maybe I was a drug user … Or maybe I wasn't committed. It gets attributed as a personality or a work ethic issue, you know? And I know that anybody can have that if you've got a health condition, but then layer that with all these other things that we've been talking about where you're vulnerable as a casual employee, or as a contract employee.

Others said the flexibility of research had allowed them to manage their health conditions, for example by doing work at night so they could attend medical appointments during the day; or being supported to take leave when needed.

As we described in Chapter 1, changing structures of university employment means there are a growing number of researchers who commence PhDs later in life, and who, despite having worked on contract for many years, are unlikely to be converted to a tenured position. This situation is especially problematic for older researchers as they are subject to a general reluctance to hire older workers. In part this is because of the system of patronage that characterises hiring decisions (e.g. doctoral supervisors will tend to hire their own students first). There is research to suggest that the further away you are from your PhD, the harder it can be to maintain a contract research career (Bosanquet et al. 2017) because your key supporters (such as supervisors) may no longer be employed at your institution. This was the case for many researchers we talked with whose supervisors had retired, changed universities or passed away. These events left researchers in particularly vulnerable situations.

Employment conditions and entitlements for older workers are also a serious financial issue and may impact on the ability to fund a reasonable retirement. As Jill said:

> [Tenured staff] get their superannuation[2] but at my age ... at my age... why can't that happen to me as well?
>
> My death [insurance cover] is like half or something. And I said, "why is that?" And he said, "because you're not full-time". You don't know [that when you start on contract].
>
> ... And if you look for any of the salary sacrifice options ... like one man who works in that research institute, said, "Oh, I claim [car parking] as a fringe benefit [tax deduction]". His car parking! So he just keeps his receipt and then he just puts it all in and he can reduce his taxable income ... I went to do it, but no. It's only for full-time people, isn't it? All these other things ...

Thinking about the minimal opportunities she (and her peers) had to ongoing work after the age of 40, Amelia went on to say:

> I just think to myself, "You know what? I'm 45 I want to retire one day". ... I don't care at this point in time what it is, provided I like the people I work with and it's consistent and I'm not expected to work every weekend. I'm getting too old for this.

Many of these workers were not only concerned with themselves and their ability to continue to find work and fund a reasonable retirement. They also worried about younger generations of researchers. Amelia called this a serious policy problem. Despite (or perhaps because of) his own situation, Charles said:

> I'm lucky in the way that I'm not in my 30s, I think that I'd be stressed out like hell, I really would be. It's stressful enough but being in your 20s and 30s to come across something like [these working conditions]. I just can't imagine what that's like, I feel so sorry for the younger people now, especially young academics and people doing their PhDs in their 30s ... I think a lot of them are going to be burnt out by my age, truly I do.

The lack of access to equal entitlements despite having worked in the sector for considerable periods of time is a worry, and one we take up in Chapter 4 where we consider how collective activism is important in removing these inequities. Clearly, the nature of these arrangements will be different in different settings, but Jill's point is important. All too often contract researchers are not fully aware of the disadvantages they are subject to. We hope the stories of Jill, Mark, Amelia and others in this book might help you to understand your rights and entitlements, and, ultimately, to add to the collective voice calling for greater equality. The nature of precarious academic work is extremely problematic as researchers age. Charles' experiences of maintaining a research career (see Vignette 2.4) provides a glimpse into the compounding effects of precarity for older researchers.

Vignette 2.4: Precarious employment for ageing researchers: Charles' story

Charles, a researcher approaching his 60s, had come to academic research late in his career. He had worked in a range of professional jobs, many of which included a research component (for example at government agencies), before undertaking his PhD. Offers of work had dwindled after the death of his doctoral supervisors. He believed many academics were hesitant to employ an older worker; preferring to help younger academics establish their careers:

> Whereas people who get to my age, typically they own their own home, they don't have any debts left ... And I guess in a way, to some people I probably am privileged but I'm not privileged in terms of having a lot of money left over, I just exist, I'm on an unemployment allowance and its honestly so tough to live on it but I do, I just manage it. It actually goes up after 60 so even the government recognises that you know, after 60, you may as well just forget it really, but I get through, just.

Charles went on to explain that despite a long career in research, he was now required to undertake Work for the Dole—an Australian scheme in which jobseekers are asked to undertake work in order to gain purportedly valuable work experience that might help them access paid employment. According to the Australian government, 'it is a work experience programme which places job seekers in activities where they can build new skills, experience and confidence to move from welfare to work while giving back to their community' (Australian Government n.d.).

> Charles: They've now got Work for the Dole for people of my age, I'm doing it at the moment actually. It doesn't give you any skills, it doesn't give you any training.
>
> Interviewer: Is it in a specific area?
>
> Charles: Well this is at a nursing home actually ... and I go and play Scrabble there with a couple of people a couple of days a week. But there's no training, there's nothing I can take to an employer, I can't go to an employer and say, 'oh, I'm good at playing Scrabble'.

Not only was this experience unlikely to help Charles access research work, but it contributed to his fragile sense of academic identity:

> ... the funny thing is, with this voluntary work—so-called voluntary work—you know, there are former academics [living] in that place ... they know [one of my former supervisors and colleagues ... It] was kind of awkward because there is this guy, one of them who lives there ... and they were all told that this guy with a PhD—me—was going to turn up and be a volunteer and they were sort of saying, "well what's wrong? What's wrong with him?" They thought that people who did community work are people who are being punished ...

Charles returned to his feelings of humiliation and grief throughout his interview, lamenting his inability to find work, to contribute to the work he loved, and having to explain his situations to others. On numerous occasions he posed the rhetorical question, 'what's wrong with me', or wondered if others thought, 'what is wrong with this guy?' Charles believed that not being offered work because of his age would likely mean early retirement:

> ... you have to pretty much accept that, that's the end of your career, you know. And the closer to 60 I get, because I'm 58 this year, the more that I have to think, "well perhaps it's true, maybe it really is close to the end of my useful working life", I just have to accept it.
>
> [Politicians] want to raise [retirement age] to 70 of all things. And you say, well

> these people must live in a cave, they must be totally out of touch if they don't realise that even by the time you're 50, even 45, people think that you've got no future left. I'm approaching 60, so I feel as though that's really my biggest problem.
>
> No one has ever said to me by the way, you're too old, never happened. Although I did go to a job agency once, I got an interview and the woman who was interviewing me said that the client she was working for, had never employed anybody over the age of 40 and to her credit, she looked appalled. I felt appalled but she looked appalled, so I think that I was thankful that she was straight up and honest with me. She didn't actually say to me, "you're too old", but the implication was pretty easy to work out and as it happened of course, I didn't get it, so that didn't surprise me.

Charles lamented not only his financial reality, but also his inability to apply the research skills he had spent decades acquiring, saying 'it makes me sad because I've had some great jobs in the past'. He went on to say:

> It's really hard, whereas a lot of people my age, they do own their own homes, they don't have debts, but still, I don't want to sit at home and do nothing at

> the same time, I just want a little bit of recognition, you know, a little bit of doing something. If I could just do, like I said, two or three days or four days, that'd be perfect, I wouldn't worry, life would be paradise if I could do that. A contract for six months, one after the other—perfect! I don't mind, that'd be good, I think it would make me a very happy person.

Moving beyond contract research

As we described above, many people who commence contract research do so with a long-term research or academic career in mind. Contracts are often seen as a stepping-stone towards permanency. However, as the literature (see Chapter 1) suggests, the number of permanent research positions (in universities and governments) is vastly outstripped by the number of PhD graduates, which can lead to a state of *permanent impermanence*. Reflecting on her decision to undertake a PhD and agree to casual research contracts Emma said:

> Ideally [when I finished my PhD I would have gotten a] research job. Or a full research and teaching academic job. That would have been perfect. That is what I aimed for. I applied for numerous jobs when I finished.

For many researchers, entering into any form of employment contract can create a sense that there is also an implicit 'psychological contract' (Rousseau 2001) with their university. The notion of psychological contracts recognises that even without a formalised contract, both employees and employers bring expectations to the work relationship. An expectation of future employment clearly does not constitute a psychological contract—this also requires the presence of associated considerations such as the exchange of hard work, stated or unstated promises of future employment and advancement. Rousseau's (1989, p. 124) seminal definition is that 'when an individual perceives that contributions he or she makes obligate the organization to reciprocity (or vice versa), a psychological contract emerges ... it is the individual's belief in an obligation of reciprocity that constitutes the contract'.

Many contract researchers we talked to described an expectation that undertaking higher degree studies alongside contract research work would ultimately lead to an opportunity for longer-term employment and promotion. Yet the tenured academics and administrators employing contract researchers are likely to have more immediate expectations around the delivery of work for existing projects, with minimal regard (or capacity) for meeting the expectations of individuals. Many researchers who embark on contract work experience a mismatch between their expectations and institutional views of reciprocity. For researchers who have taken on work and higher degree studies (such as a PhD) with this expectation (and are subsequently unable to achieve tenured employment), this path almost inevitably leads to a sense of a breach of the psychological contract. While some researchers are content to continue in contract positions for different reasons (such as wanting flexibility so they can work around the demands of young families), many would prefer to move into more permanent academic work. Yet many in this group remain in contract positions because they are unable to find or attain tenured research-only positions.

Exposure to academia can also create disillusionment with academic employment more broadly: for example, tenured early career academic positions often require significant hours, and may also comprise a reasonably heavy teaching component. These positions can therefore also be perceived as an equally unattractive alternative. Commenting on excessive hours, Emma said:

> the workload for academics is just insane. The jobs that you would get ... and you think this when you're casual ... the jobs that you would get if you could get a job ... it would be awful. Just look at them!

The disjuncture between earlier hopes and dreams of academic work and lived realities can mean making difficult decisions about the career path. For those who are hoping to move into academic careers, however, understanding the nature of academic work and job applications and expectations is vitally important.

Tenured academic job applications

Pitt and Mewburn's (2016, p. 99) analysis of academic job advertisements in Australia reveals that the 'new academic ... is a multi-talented, always ready and available worker that we have started to label the *academic superhero*, capable of being everything to everyone and leaping over 24 Key Selection Criteria in a single job application'.

While contract research positions are often not advertised (see above), the recruitment processes for tenured or longer fixed-term positions tend to be highly formalised (Fumasoli & Goastellec 2015). These often require responses to selection criteria, and the ability to demonstrate that you are the 'multi-talented' academic. These applications are often highly competitive and take considerable time to assemble. This creates a problem for the precariously employed worker because applying for a position means directing hours away from paid employment or dedicating personal time to developing applications. Emma said:

> The first challenge would be that I am always thinking about permanent employment and the next contract. Some of the time that I could be spending writing, I am spending writing applications. You have to do that in your own time on top of all the other stuff.

As described above, even being in a position to apply for a tenured position requires a great deal of forward planning—ensuring you have a good publication record, experience in areas such as grant writing and teaching, and so on. Blair described being disheartened at having worked hard to 'get a lot on our CV, and we can't even get interviews' for academic roles:

> And I have people read my applications, I have them make sure everything is right, that … I'm actually addressing what the university is looking for, what the department is looking for. I'm doing all of that high level work, I'm having chats with the heads of schools that are on the things, I'm doing all of that, and I still can't seem to even get an interview for roles that I might be really well suited for.

This need to be an academic superhero was also raised by Penny who said she had found that it is also increasingly common for employers to look for researchers who will 'bring something to the table'. Again, the disjuncture between institutional expectations and structures is highlighted. Penny said while many employers prefer to recruit a researcher with money (typically in the form of a research grant) and ongoing programs of research, 'you *can't* if you're not [securely] employed'.

While some researchers (such as Amy) went on to find permanent work it is a challenging prospect because of the impact applying for jobs can have on your scholarly identity, as Blair described:

> I think I get caught up in this idea that because I don't have a permanent position I must not be good enough, which is such bullshit, and it's, well I tell people that's bullshit, and I tell students that it's bullshit, but that's not what reality is ...

As we have discussed throughout this book, insecure work is emblematic of advanced liberal governance. The anxieties and ontological insecurity that were described above not only encourage individual researchers to feel responsible for their own career and financial security, but also have an impact on researchers' subjectivities. Loveday (2018, p. 161) has described the rise of the 'neurotic academic' which is 'predicated upon anxiety rather than in spite of anxiety'. Many of the researchers we talked with described themselves in terms of deficits—blaming themselves and worrying about their ability to live up to institutional expectations and norms; and explaining their successes as instances of luck. Ashley said that:

> It's quite hard on your confidence ... I went through a bit of a stage before my contract finished at one university where ... like because I'd known it was a three-year contract ... I mean both times I was like it's a three-year contract, there are no expectations for what happens after that and then the first time I felt very fortunate that I got another contract and then again the second time I was like you know no expectations. I'm not expecting there to be another contract after this but I still kind of found myself getting to a point where I'm like "Why don't they want me?" Did they think that I'm not good enough, would they find the money if they could? So I think just there's a lot of self-doubt. You're just like maybe I'm not performing enough, maybe I'm not publishing enough.

For some, this anxiety ultimately leads them to move away from a research career altogether.

Moving to non-research positions

A number of the researchers we talked with had made a decision to move away from research, and away from the pursuit of an academic position. This included moving into non-academic roles in universities (such as management and administrative positions) through to taking on further teaching work (typically casual university tutoring and lecturing), working in government organisations, and working for industrial unions. Amelia, who had experienced frustration at not being able to find ongoing research work said that:

> ... in some ways [moving out of an academic position] was the best thing that could have happened to me, because I was able to say... "I'm out of here and I'll never be back".

Since she made the decision to move into an administrative role, Amelia had been in a meeting with academic staff who were talking about why PhD researchers don't move out of academia:

> And I was just thinking to myself, and I was trying to keep the conversation going, because I wanted to know for myself, what those opportunities were.

Amelia—like many others we talked with—had a significant work history in the private sector prior to commencing her doctoral studies. She was concerned that her PhD, followed by years of temporary research employment, were now hindering her chances of finding ongoing work:

> The irony for me is, while I've always said I never did any of this for [an academic] career, it surely ... damaged any career that I could have because ... PhD work, I think it actually is a negative. People see it and they kind of go, "What is that?" My husband keeps telling me, "this is ridiculous". You know? For the money that you get ... And I go, anyone who looks at my CV is going to think, "She's too much".

This concern around PhD graduate employment has been taken up by researchers such as Mewburn et al. (2018). For contract researchers, the issue of how to access employment possibilities post-contract research (and post-PhD) were a concern. The disparate nature of work means it can be a challenge to create a cohesive job application as Amy said:

> And what do you even put on your resume? ... What I try and do is focus on the things that are of general interest. So for example, I would talk about drafting reports, dealing with a large amount of data and stakeholder engagements. Things like that. Things that are typical in any business. Because ... people see PhD or people see that you work in a university, it seems a very narrow field.

Ashley described having been in a workshop with a more senior academic who had worked in recruitment in the public sector:

> ... he kind of took me under his mentoring wing a little bit in terms of he's going, "So we need to sit down and we'll talk about your career because you think that you haven't got that many skills that are transferable but you know I definitely think you do".

This was a question we put to Raewyn Connell, who suggested that contract researchers see themselves as knowledge producers, regardless of having multiple 'jobs' (contracts). She suggested that 'that's your job; you're a knowledge producer'.

A final word

Despite their position in a seemingly prestigious world of scholarly work (the so-called 'ivory tower'), many contract researchers are unable to access conditions that were previously taken for granted—from employment entitlements such as holidays, sick pay, work security and a sense of being an integral part of the institution. This situation has increased the power differential between employers and contract researchers, who remain vulnerable as the supply of qualified candidates exceeds the number of tenured academic positions in universities. Often, researchers internalise what they perceive as their own 'failures'.

The possibilities for unequal and exploitative working conditions are exacerbated by the reality that hiring decisions are not only short-term, but also made by individuals in a profession that has traditionally been self-governing. Creating and sustaining a network of ethical colleagues to work with is vitally important. The vignette that follows (see Vignette 2.5) provides a reflection on the essential nature of building networks of trusted colleagues:

Vignette 2.5: Blog: Finding a balance when working on somebody else's projects

Finding a balance when working on somebody else's projects (Harris & Spina 2017)

In the post that prompted our contribution, Pat described some of the ethical and political issues associated with working as a contracted researcher. But there are other challenges that arise when working on 'soft money', which only seem to be talked about in shared offices or quiet, snatched conversations involving coffee or wine.

Counting the time before, after and during our PhDs, between the two of us we have been employed as part of what Kimber (2003) described as the 'tenuous periphery' for almost two decades and have experienced many challenges and opportunities in working on other people's projects. Our post focuses on doing contract research post-PhD. Simultaneously balancing PhD research with paid research work deserves a whole blog post of its own!

The first hurdle that contract researchers face is finding suitable work. Word-of-mouth is king in the world of contract research. Aside from the coveted three-year project manager or research fellow positions, short-term research work is rarely advertised. Getting your foot in the door and doing good work is key to the next contract. Academics talk, and good researchers are a highly prized commodity.

The dark side of this esteem is the need to self-regulate. Because of the precarious nature of short-term contracts, researchers often accept work whenever it is available. Gathering stores for the proverbial winter. It is not uncommon to see researchers employed for more than 40 hours a week, on multiple contracts taken back to back in fear that the next contract might not appear. For some researchers, this can continue for years without break. The system is fuelled by our desire to engage in high-quality research, to achieve continuing employment, and our need to pay the bills.

The nature and pace of this work is dramatically different from doctoral research. During the PhD, you are encouraged to take time to ponder new ideas or immerse yourself in the literature. Every aspect of your work is subject to scrutiny from supervisors and examiners. Moving on from that experience, it can be tricky to limit yourself to the time dictated by a contract if it feels like it is not enough to produce quality work. We have both had the experience of working additional (unpaid) hours to complete work, worried that we might be seen as working too slowly, or that our work is not good enough. We make these decisions fully aware that research budgets often won't stretch to cover more hours and that the academics who have employed us also face workload pressures.

While many of these concerns are tied up with our identity as researchers, the pressure is intensified when you are competing with others and hoping to increase your chances of another contract, or an ongoing position.

The dreaded 'imposter syndrome' never seems to be far from researchers, and those working on short-term contracts are certainly not immune. You are thrown into the deep end, often using methods or working on projects that are outside or—if you are lucky—on the periphery of your field. The learning curve for any new project is steep. As any researcher working on multiple projects knows, it is tricky to keep track of all the associated details.

The ability to engage in ongoing and focused programs of research and deepen your expertise in a particular field is a luxury that is not available when working on other people's projects. You tend to take on projects that are interesting but not necessarily related to your previous research. After a while, your publication record might end up a bit patchy—or worse—which isn't helpful when looking for tenured work. Finding time to write from the thesis can take a back seat to the immediate pressures of research work. While you might review the literature, transcribe interviews, code data, and undertake preliminary analyses, contract researchers are far less likely to be paid to write publications or to be named on publications that use their work.

It sounds like we are saying that working on somebody else's project is a terrible idea. On the contrary, working on others' projects can open opportunities and benefits that are not accessible in other ways. Working on projects that are led by others builds experience and expertise across a range of areas while you are supported by experienced researchers. The focus of a PhD limits researchers from engaging with a wide range of topics and methods. Working on other projects helps researchers to move beyond the familiar.

Despite the insecurity and uncertainty of contract research work, personally, this type of work has helped to us both to develop networks, find mentoring relationships, build collaborative research relationships and grow in confidence. And importantly for us, 'working on other people's projects' is how we met!

This type of work provides experience and support in navigating some of the tricky aspects of conducting research before you start taking ownership of projects yourself. While you might contribute excellent research to a project, you don't have the weight of large-scale studies and meeting institutional requirements solely on your shoulders. If the

> financial uncertainties and performance pressures of contract research could be alleviated, this type of work might allow researchers to find flexible employment and a brilliant training ground.
>
> We think it is important to tease out these discussions and consider the question of how can we, in both the 'tenured core' and the 'tenuous periphery', overcome the challenges and uncertainties to support better opportunities for contract researchers.

Notes

1 We have used the term *lead researchers* as a catch-all term for the person who is ostensibly in charge of the research or project. Different jurisdictions and institutions use different terms such as Principal Investigator or Chief Investigator.
2 Superannuation in Australia is a compulsory system where a minimum percentage of income is invested to fund retirement. It is partly compulsory, but further encouraged by tax benefits. University employees in Australia typically hold accounts with UniSuper, and the nature of employment can impact on the superannuation products that are available, as well as the rate of employer contribution. In this case, Jill is comparing the 17% superannuation contribution made for tenured academics with the 9% contribution for casual employees (who are obviously also paid at substantially lower rates of pay).

References

Allan, K., 2019, 'Volunteering as hope labour: The potential value of unpaid work experience for the un-and under-employed culture', *Theory and Critique*, vol. 60, no. 1, pp. 66–83.

Alvesson, M. & Spicer, A., 2016, '(Un)conditional surrender? Why do professionals willingly comply with managerialism', *Journal of Organizational Change Management*, vol. 29, no. 1, pp. 29–45.

Australian Government. (n.d.). *Work for the Dole*. Retrieved from https://jobsearch.gov.au/jobs/work-for-the-dole.

Ball, S.J., 2000, 'Performativities and fabrications in the education economy: Towards the performative society?', *The Australian Educational Researcher*, vol. 27, no. 2, pp. 1–23.

Baranay, I., 2013, 'The academic underclass: The plight of casual teaching staff', in J Schultz; (ed), 2006, *Getting Smart: The Battle for Ideas in Education*, Griffith Review, no. 11, pp. 39–49.

Bosanquet, A., Mailey, A., Matthews, K.E. & Lodge, J.M., 2017, 'Redefining "early career" in academia: A collective narrative approach', *Higher Education Research & Development*, vol. 36, no. 5, pp. 890–902, doi: 10. 1080/07294360.2016.1263934.

Bourdieu, P., 1988, *Homo Academicus*, Stanford: Stanford University Press.

Bröckling, U., 2015, *The Entrepreneurial Self: Fabricating a New Type of Subject*, Thousand Oaks: Sage.

Brown, T., Goodman, J. & Yasukawa, K., 2010, 'Academic casualization in Australia: Class divisions in the university', *Journal of Industrial Relations*, vol. 52, no. 2, pp. 169–182, doi: 10.1177/0022185609359443.

Cannizzo, F., 2018, '"You've got to love what you do": Academic labour in a culture of authenticity', *The Sociological Review*, vol. 66, no. 1, pp. 91–106.

Clance, P.R. & Imes, S.A., 1978, 'The imposter phenomenon in high achieving women: Dynamics and therapeutic intervention', *Psychotherapy: Theory, Research & Practice*, vol. 15, no. 3, pp. 241–247.

Cochran-Smith, M., 2012, 'Composing a research life', *Action in Teacher Education*, vol. 34, no. 2, pp. 99–110.

Coin, F., 2018, 'When love becomes self-abuse: Gendered perspectives on unpaid labor in academia', in Y Taylor and K Lahad (eds), *Feeling Academic in the Neoliberal University*, Cham, SUI: Palgrave Macmillan. pp. 301–320.

Edwards, D., Bexley, E. & Richardson, S., 2011, *Regenerating the Academic Workforce: The Careers, Intentions and Motivations of Higher Degree Research Students in Australia. Findings of the National Research Student Survey (NRSS)*, Melbourne: Australian Council for Educational Research, https://research.acer.edu.au/higher_education/23/, accessed 7 March 2018.

Fumasoli, T. & Goastellec, G., 2015, 'Global models, disciplinary and local patterns in academic recruitment processes', in T. Fumasoli, G. Goastellec and B. Kehm (eds), *Academic Work and Careers in Europe: Trends, Challenges, Perspectives*, Cham: Springer. pp. 69–93.

Giddens, A., 1991, *Modernity and Self-Identity: Self and Society in the Late Modern Age*, Cambridge, UK: Polity Press.

Gregg, M., 2017, 'Banal Bohemia: Blogging from the ivory tower hotdesk', *Convergence: The International Journal of Research into New Media Technologies*, vol. 15, no. 4, pp. 470–483, 2009.

Gruber, T., 2014, 'Academic sell-out: How an obsession with metrics and rankings is damaging academia', *Journal of Marketing for Higher Education*, vol. 24, no. 2, pp. 165–177.

Harney, B., Monks, K., Alexopoulos, A., Buckley, F. & Hogan, T., 2014, 'University research scientists as knowledge workers: Contract status and employment opportunities', *International Journal of Human Resource Management*, vol. 25, no. 16, pp. 2219–2233, doi: 10.1080/09585192. 2011.561241.

Hayot, E., 2014, *The Elements of Academic Style: Writing for the Humanities*, Columbia, MA: Columbia University Press.

Ivancheva, M.P., 2015, 'The age of precarity and the new challenges to the academic profession', *Studia Europaea*, vol. 60, no. 1, pp. 39–47.

Loveday, V., 2018, 'The neurotic academic: Anxiety, casualisation, and governance in the neoliberalising university', *Journal of Cultural Economy*, vol. 11, no. 2, pp. 154–166.

Lynch-Biniek, A., 2017, 'Don't rock the boat: Curricular choices of contingent and permanent composition faculty', *Academic Labor: Research and Artistry*, vol. 1, no. 1, pp. 15–30.

Marsh, S., 2018, 'Chanel shoes, but no salary: How one woman exposed the scandal of the French fashion industry', *The Guardian*, www.theguardian.com/fashion/2018/sep/02/academic-exposing-ugly-reality-high-fashion-giulia-mensitieri?CMP=share_btn_link, accessed 4 July 2019.

Mensitieri, G., 2012, *The Most Beautiful Job in the World*, Paris: La Découverte.

Mewburn, I., 2017, *How to Be an Academic*, Sydney: New South Publishing.

Mewburn, I., Grant, W.J., Suominen, H. & Kizimchuk, S., 2018, 'A machine learning analysis of the non-academic employment opportunities for PhD graduates in Australia', *Higher Education Policy*, pp. 1–15. doi: 10.1057/s41307-018-0098-4.

Nadolny, A. & Ryan, S., 2015, 'McUniversities revisited: A comparison of university and McDonald's casual employee experiences in Australia', *Studies in Higher Education*, vol. 40, no. 1, pp. 142–157.

Nikolaidis, E. & Maroudas, L., 2013, 'Institutional changes and the expansion of flexible forms of employment in higher education: The case of Greek universities', *Journal for Critical Education Policy Studies (JCEPS)*, vol. 11, no. 3, pp. 127–145.

Pitt, R. & Mewburn, I., 2016, 'Academic superheroes? A critical analysis of academic job descriptions', *Journal of Higher Education Policy and Management*, vol. 38, no. 1, pp. 88–101.

Pocock, B., 2003, *The Work/Life Collision: What Work is Doing to Australians and What to Do about It*, Sydney: Federation Press.

Ritzer, G., 1993, *The Macdonaldization of Society*, London: Pine Forge Press.

Rousseau, D.M., 1989, 'Psychological and implied contracts in organizations', *Employee Responsibilities and Rights Journal*, vol. 2, no. 2, pp. 121–139.

Rousseau, D.M., 2001, 'Schema, promise and mutuality: The building blocks of the psychological contract', *Journal of Occupational and Organizational Psychology*, vol. 74, no. 4, pp. 511–541.

Sang, K., Powell, A., Finkel, R. & Richards, J., 2015, '"Being an academic is not a 9–5 job": Long working hours and the "ideal worker" in UK academia', *Labour & Industry: A Journal of the Social and Economic Relations of Work*, vol. 25, no. 3, pp. 235–249, doi: 10.1080/10301763.2015.1081723.

Standing, G., 2011, *The Precariat—The New Dangerous Class*, London: Bloomsbury.

Sword, H., 2017, *Air & Light & Time & Space: How Successful Academics Write*, Harvard: Harvard University Press.

Thomson, P. & Kamler, B., 2013, *Writing for Peer Reviewed Journals: Strategies for Getting Published*, Milton Park: Routledge.

3 The collective work of contract research

Collegiality, not competition

Research ideas don't spring out of nowhere. We only know about current controversies in our field, what is worth researching, or what is doable by reading journals and talking to others. I must confess that I don't have time to read many research articles, and without a clear purpose in mind, why would I? I read most and most effectively when I'm working on a proposal or paper, because then I know what I'm looking for. So expecting people to leisurely browse peer-reviewed journals when they're balancing multiple research projects might be unrealistic. That leaves talking to others. Those in less research-intensive universities might not have many active researchers in their departments, so being able to attend conferences becomes even more important as a way of networking and staying in touch with one's discipline.

Universities should make time and funding available for conference attendance even if staff are not yet ready to present. Ideally,

this funding should take the form of a budget for each person, not an ever-decreasing pot of money that staff are forced to compete against their colleagues for. Those who are less research active are likely to be less experienced in applying for funding, so are disadvantaged by a competitive system of internal research funding. And anyway, it's **collegiality we need, not more competition**.
—Reflections of a contract researcher

In this chapter, we argue that collectivising strategies, developed and enacted by researchers and other stakeholders, are the best means through which more productive and predictable working conditions for contract researchers can be forged in the current context. At present, most strategies for supporting productive and predictable working conditions tend to focus on what researchers can do to help themselves (Broadbent & Strachan 2016; Harney et al. 2014). We do not want to place increasing pressure on contract researchers in addition to their invisible and unpaid labour but we recognise that collective strategies are required to create supportive workplaces for all researchers. This chapter focuses on the importance of collectivisation for work and career building. Collectivising strategies provide important professional, emotional and practical support to researchers at all levels, from those just entering the field to the most experienced professors. When researchers establish collaborative strategies, they can generate a sense of belonging that is often absent in traditional structures for contract researchers (Bryson & Barnes 2000).

Employment on other people's projects

Contract research is not an individual endeavour. One of the key difficulties associated with finishing a PhD (which is primarily a solo endeavour) and entering the world of contract research is the need to work with others and on other academics' projects. As described in Chapter 2, this transition is often accompanied by an identity shift from contract researcher to an agile and entrepreneurial researcher. The work of a PhD requires doctoral candidates to become experts in their field (Park 2007), to develop and independently undertake research and to learn to write independently under the supervision of an academic adviser (Deuchar 2008). As Pat Thomson writes:

> Having done their own independent piece of research, supported by a supervisor, they then find themselves generating most of the data on someone else's project, doing first-cut analysis and drafting texts, working to someone else's research design and someone else's research practices. It's as if they'd had *L plates* on for a long time, briefly took them off and then had to put them right back on again.
> (Thomson 2017, p. 3)

Being contracted to work on other people's projects often means working in a field that is not always directly aligned with your field of expertise. Contract researchers often, if not almost always, need to work on projects that have been conceptualised, designed and, sometimes, had data collected by others. Bridget, herself an experienced contract researcher, suggests the ideal candidate is someone who can 'keep your head down, you get publications, but you don't have your own research. You are research-for-hire'.

This identity as research-for-hire can be challenging for contract researchers who have been trained to undertake research in particular methods or theoretical traditions. Green and Turok (2000) indicate that flexibility and adaptability are sought-after commodities within the contingent labour force. Despite previous experience, you are unlikely to be in control of study design, methods, processes and analysis and so required to adapt to designs that have been previously conceptualised. Some contract researchers can feel that this is a step backwards, from a position as a leader of research to a position that has minimal control over research direction, design or implementation. As Therese said:

> It's not your project. So you don't determine the direction, they do; you don't determine anything, you just do what you're told.

Contract researchers' work is directed by lead researchers, who are generally tenured academics. If your research disciplinary interests, methods and approaches align, it can be a happy and productive experience. When this occurs, your work will not only be intellectually engaging, it will also provide you with the opportunity to contribute to a project that is beyond the scope of what an individual researcher could conduct. Research on larger projects, related to your own field, can extend your expertise; allowing you to flex your methodological and theoretical muscles. Hey (2001) suggests that the acceleration and quantification of research outputs means that contract researchers have significant power in this setting, due to the intellectual capital they bring to organisations. However, as described in Chapter 2, reading, writing and researching in a new discipline or tradition can be challenging, and time-consuming. This is not to say that these opportunities might not be rewarding. Rachel, for example, found working with families of very sick children to be highly rewarding, despite this work being very different from her previous work. Despite it being a new field, this position afforded many opportunities to learn, contribute and travel (including to overseas conferences).

Conversely, you might be asked to manage a project that does not fit your ideas of research design, or to analyse data in unfamiliar ways. While this can be uncomfortable, it can give you the opportunity to learn new approaches. Flexibility in research can also afford the opportunity to develop innovative ways of thinking about and managing research projects (Allen-Collinson & Hockey 1998). As Hey (2001, p. 81) states 'if we consider (and I do) that collaborative teams produce better theory and better work? They are also likely to be better at developing people's skills and capacities as well'. Working on research that has been previously conceptualised by others, however, can require considerable skill to ensure that research follows a plan. As Paula describes:

> we were a bit limited in our scope. We couldn't kind of go "This is how we think it should run" we'd have to say, "This is how we said it's going to run, how do we make that happen?"

This situation is common for contract researchers who are often employed after projects have been developed and when key design features are no longer negotiable. As McCulloch (2017, p. 7) reports 'Some may worry that, as a researcher on someone else's project, they won't be able to pursue their own research agenda. This is up for negotiation, however'. Even when major design decisions have been finalised, there can still be spaces to make your own contribution, such as analysing data using your preferred theoretical approach, and taking the lead on writing up and publishing your analysis with your team. This was an approach Rachel took to her career:

> I think what really helps is that you're able to adapt and move into different teams. One thing I always tried to encourage was writing publications because that also enables you to get external feedback on your own work as well …
>
> So if you can build your own little track record, even though you're probably not really in control of the projects, or managing and designing them.

Because Rachel's expertise is quantitative analysis, she is typically employed after projects have been designed and funded. However, as she points out, being willing to work within the confines of an existing project can support researchers to build skills in a range of areas from writing to building collaborative relationships with industry partners; and negotiating the conduct of effective research practices. That said, we acknowledge the significant structural barriers for contract researchers as they attempt to develop a sustained program of research while jumping between disparate research projects that have been designed by others.

Quality research: balancing independence and collegiality

> You learn along the way to ask as many questions as possible but it is kind of hard to do

> that when you're just starting out and you have no confidence and you kind of want to look like you know what you are doing. But I guess through that process, I've learned that you always need to send emails really getting the who, what, when, where and why are we doing this piece of research.
>
> —Danielle

When asked what they look for in employing contract researchers, the head of a large research team reported:

> there's obviously skills and experience and capacity to work effectively fairly independently, and then balancing that with looking for people who are open to criticism, advice, guidance and so on. So there's some balancing I think between those two things.

Being able to contribute to research is not just about the individual contract researcher; it is a collective endeavour that relies on the contributions of every member of the team to balance key accountabilities, their emotional labour and build collective research identities (Wilson & Holligan 2013). Experienced contract researchers and employers we talked to agreed that striking a balance between independence, quality of work and collegiality was important. In addition to being able to work independently, researchers agreed that being able to work collaboratively (and decipher the needs of employing researchers) was essential. Kathy said that finding work '[has] got to do with quality and … and [finding] somebody that they can work with'. Charles' comments were also typical of the need to produce quality work while being a supportive and collaborative colleague. He said:

> I think the first thing is that people have to do quality work ... in our research environment in particular, is being able to be part of a team. If you can't be part of a team, and our team in particular, then it's—you're not going to stay here very long ... So we have a really supportive environment that—where our research-people all support each other, and we're all working towards a common goal ... there's no judgement if you are all about your career and it's about you, I don't judge that if that's what you want to do as a researcher, then that's fine. But I don't think you've got a place in our team ... Because we work as a team, together, to move the whole research centre forward.

Charles' comments highlight the importance of quality work and a collegiate approach not just for purposes of getting the next contract, but also to make work an enjoyable experience for all.

One of the more difficult elements of this collegial work, however, was reported to be balancing the need to clarify team expectations with working independently and proficiently. Chris described his experiences:

> Being an independent worker is really, really useful as well. If you can't work independently ... if one of the people in the team I manage ... I've got a few projects, but if I'm getting five or six emails a day from somebody just checking small little things like ... make a goddamn decision and move on ...
>
> Go and look for the answer before you come and ask somebody and go 'Look, I can't find

> it'. Yep, that's fine, there's no stupid questions but you just have to ... I spend a lot of time answering stupid questions.

As Chris indicates, while seeking clarification and feedback is important, there is an underlying value placed on independence and self-regulation. Academics and contract researchers are busy and unlikely to have the time or energy to spend on supporting an inefficient researcher, creating a complex situation in which researchers are both required to work within strict confines of a project design and hold the 'core values of autonomy and self-regulation' (Wilson & Holligan 2013, p. 228).

This complex working environment is part of what our participants described as being a responsible researcher. The ability to complete work independently, work with others when needed and to provide high-quality outputs and contributions is essential because it means academics will feel more comfortable re-employing you or referring you to colleagues. Underpinning the discussion of collegiality and independence is the consistent understanding of a need to produce high-quality work at all times. While few doctoral programs in the Social Sciences and Humanities train researchers to work on collaborative projects, the ongoing performative pressure works to establish this notion of the 'academic superhero'. As Chris said:

> My goal is to do a great job all the time ... But, having said that, there is a layer of pressure to always ... you feel like you always have to prove yourself, I guess ... Yeah, it's like this continual ... otherwise you may not get the [next] job.

Ethical dilemmas

While deciphering and meeting project needs is important, in Chapter 4 we also consider how institutions might support researchers to meet these expectations in fairer ways. A worrying trend in our data was the number of researchers we talked to who described having worked on projects where their own standards of research quality and ethics were being compromised. Some of the stories we heard included researchers being asked to delete research data or being asked to withhold results from research participants (as promised in ethics applications), along with stories of unethical hiring and firing, racism and bullying. Rachel said:

> … I had these two projects that were back-to-back, where the team and the management was just hugely dysfunctional. Quite nice people if you just met them at an event or something, but an absolute nightmare to work with. Unfortunately, in those situations all you can do is try and protect your own reputation, just do what you're asked to do, unless it's something really wrong, then don't do it obviously. Avoid publishing or representing anything with those people, and just try and get yourself into something else where you can build your publication record.

Penny described her experiences of being asked to compromise research quality and ethics by saying that 'you are the face of the project, yet you have absolutely no control over what goes. That's probably one of the hardest things, is that you don't have any control'. We contend that the extent of precarity in research employment creates a serious power imbalance that requires much deeper consideration by universities, research institutes and funding bodies—this is an issue we take up further in Chapter 4. We conclude this section with Laura's story (Vignette 3.1), who like Rachel, took a personal risk to maintain her own integrity.

> ## Vignette 3.1: Laura's experience of research quality and ethics
>
> Laura had significant experience in research in a number of settings—from community groups to universities and government departments. As a highly committed researcher, she had numerous concerns around working on projects that adopted practices that she knew to be unethical. A major dilemma for Laura was meeting her own ethical standards (alongside university and national standards for ethical research), while balancing the power dynamics of being precariously employed. She said:
>
>> One of the really serious by-products [of precarious research employment] is ethics and forcing people to be compliant in situations where you can't be.
>
> She went on to describe a project where one of her first tasks was to conduct research interviews with children. Laura had been brought

onto the project after it had already commenced. The project was already running behind schedule, so the Chief Investigator was keen for the interviews to be conducted as soon as possible. Understanding the importance of informed consent when working with minors, Laura asked to see signed written consent forms. Laura said she was told:

> "You don't need to see those", and I thought, that's a very odd response for having to work with minors, you know? And I said, "What do you mean?"

Laura went on to explain that time pressures to undertake interviews without any evidence of informed consent meant that she felt 'shut out' of ethical processes. Against the instructions of her immediate supervisor, Laura decided that her own personal ethics and duty of care required her to seek written consent via email. She said:

> It cost me, it cost me big time ... So, I did that for two years. And that entire time, he refused to let me see consent forms ...

As Laura's account indicates, the power imbalances that characterise insecure research employment relations can have enormous implications on both quality and ethical research practices.

Feeling like you belong

Imposter syndrome is considered a characteristic of academic careers (Knights & Clarke 2014). Our interviews illustrate that there is a shared sense amongst researchers working on fixed-term or casual contracts that they do not feel that they are valued, included or viewed as full members of the academic community.

One of the institutionalised practices that contributes to contract researchers not feeling like full members of the academic community is the limited space for research work. The massification of higher education and the growth in the number of academics hired in the university over the past three decades has resulted in physical limitations in university buildings. While work in the sciences often includes multiple researchers working in shared labs, contract researchers in other fields are increasingly required to 'hot-desk', work from home, or find space in communal areas to complete their work. The itinerant nature of contract work contrasts with lecturers, who often have their own office. Heather said:

> If I came [to campus] to work … I didn't have a desk. I didn't have anywhere to go. I'd sit in the library or whatever. If I needed to be, or was here, early before teaching or something and I wanted to do some work on something, I just had to go find a space. There wasn't really anywhere to be necessarily. So that was just probably a symbolic thing, I guess.

The spatial dynamic was raised by numerous researchers and was often coupled by other, less visible, forms of exclusion. For example, contract researchers may not be included on academic email lists or be invited to staff meetings, which can result in those on short-term contracts feeling like outsiders. Furthermore, the lack of full academic membership in meetings or emails mean that contract researchers are not formally able to access information about strategic organisational matters and activities in the university. Their knowledge is often restricted to the local teams in which they work. This marginalisation has also been documented elsewhere in the literature. For example, Loveday (2018, p. 159) provides the example of a senior researcher who avoided a departmental day because 'I just did not know whether to come or not'; and another who felt like 'a real loser' because she had to work out of a colleague's office space. Once again, we argue that these institutional structures have a significant impact on the psychological wellbeing and employment prospects of researchers and must be brought to the attention of employers.

Writing on other people's projects

As Laura's comment in Chapter 2 indicated, contract researchers often 'work full-time ... but [are] not *considered* a full-time staff member', meaning that many of the industrial entitlements for permanent employees are not available, despite working full-time hours. While it is important to familiarise yourself with your industrial entitlements, it is also important that you understand your rights as a researcher when working with others. A recurring problem for many contract researchers is their inclusion (and acknowledgement) on publications.

As described in Chapter 2, work required in short-term contracts can include time to spend on writing papers—one of the key performance indicators that supports moves into continuing research employment. Rather than leading publications, however, contract researchers are often employed to assist with writing through developing literature reviews or conducting some elements of analysis. Even when contract researchers are included in publication writing teams—sometimes doing so on an unpaid basis—a related issue is the difficulty of resuming analytic thinking after being immersed in the predominantly administrative tasks that are often required of contract researchers. Amy said:

> It's a huge brain switch and it's a huge identity switch in some ways to go from managing research teams and organising research teams and keeping good document ... paths or trails, managing the ethics or whatever it might be. Switching from that to thinking, "oh right, I'm also a researcher that could be contributing to the brainwork, to the deep thinking about this project". It's almost like I'm a bit split so I often find that just ... I don't know. I don't know why but I often find that I just fall back into that admin kind of side.

Because so much of the everyday experiences of contract staff includes data collection and project management within clear guidelines, maintaining an identity as a scholar who engages in analysis and writing can be a challenge. When writing is part of your employment, this work is often subsumed by more immediate needs of those in the research team. Amy went on to say:

> Those administrative type tasks that have a deadline or have people waiting for them,

they're always going to be the first priorities but they're not necessarily the tasks that end up with rich rewards on the research side. But still they have to be done.

Short-term involvement in research and writing can mean that you may not be working on the paper long enough to see it through to publication. Heather had been on a project where she had been involved in recruiting research participants, collecting and analysing data, and writing. She had completed writing for two papers, one that had been submitted and rejected (by the first journal it was submitted to); and another that was still under review. Unfortunately, Heather moved on to a new contract, which created a level of complexity that tenured academics would not typically have to negotiate:

> ... I submitted them before I left but ... so I've got to re-submit, but now I've kind of got another job. I just haven't got back to it, which I just carry guilt around for constantly. I'm like, "I *really* need to do that" but then something will come up like a job application and I'm like, "I really need to do *that*".

Contract researchers can also find that they are unable to use data from their research to develop publications. Rebecca, for example, describes the issues associated with working on industry-funded projects where the intellectual property of the research project belonged to the industry partners. That meant that despite their work, Rebecca and colleagues were extremely limited in their ability to publish throughout this large, three-year research project. As Rebecca said, the project team were easily able to meet the requirements of the funding body, but these requirements did not align with institutional publication metrics of producing a number of publications each year. She found that she was having to take on additional work and draw on data from her PhD research in order to meet publication requirements in time outside her contracted full-time employment. In business terms, this means her position was effectively limiting her ability to meet key performance indicators. She had to do additional work out-of-hours in order to meet these expectations.

Working for free

Working proactively to meet institutional or research targets can mean working for free. If a contract specifies particular tasks (such as data collection, literature reviews, field work and the like), writing is often done by contract researchers in their own time, in addition to the less visible forms of labour documented in Chapter 2. This situation can lead to difficult situations for contract researchers. Annabel, for example, reported that lead researchers informed her that her paid contributions to papers, through literature reviews and writing up analyses, meant she was not eligible to be named as an author. Unless she was contracted to a project, however, she would not be paid for any time to work on building a publication record. For many, like Annabel, the desire to build an academic career meant there was an imperative to work on publications outside of paid hours, offering unpaid contribution to papers, or working on sole-authored publications unrelated to their employment. In contemporary times, the vast majority of those in academia, from tenured to temporary, are subject to similar circumstances and struggles, required to work on publications outside paid hours. The institutionalised 'publish or perish' culture poses a substantial problem particularly for individuals in earlier career stages, regardless of their contract status. However, the use of fixed-term contract employment enacts an even more transactional relationship between individuals and institutions, which undermines the reciprocity that has traditionally been seen as balancing the psychological contract between academics and universities. In order to seek academic work, and meet publication expectations, contract researchers sometimes accept lower hours so they retain time to publish, as Jason said:

> That's why for me, the RA jobs that I've missed out on that were three days a week for 12 months, that's just for someone in my position, that's pure gold. Three days a week in a position that will actually yield some publications from that, plus, two or three days a week to finish publishing from your PhD. That's the ticket, if you can get it, as far as I can tell.

Of course, this 'pure gold' also means surviving on a part-time income. Emma discussed this issue of working in a system that actively creates an underclass of workers who cannot meet systemic demands because of institutional structures:

> It is a cycle. And you're thinking it is really short term. And at the same time, you're still trying to produce your own research. So you are like, "If I can get enough [paid] work to tide me over,

> maybe I can write my article, and once my article is published … like I have had two articles this year". So it is that sort of thing. So you don't think about the long-term prospects of actually getting a job. You just think about the next thing.

For Emma, there were economic realities tied to decisions about how she should spend her time. Because her paid employment did not allow her to pursue her goal of developing an academic identity and career, she needed to build this identity in her own time. This disconnect between institutional standards and the standards of paid employment contribute to the 'intensification and extensification' (Gill 2010, p. 234) of academic work and helps to cement the notion that you need to be an academic 'superhero' to survive. Jason, for example, talked about balancing teaching and research contracts:

> I work every weekend. I've been—this whole year I'd be lucky to have one day off a fortnight. Sometimes I'll have—I'll work two, three weeks. Three weeks without having a day where I don't do any uni work. I'm in the middle of one now because I've got guest lecture, guest lecture, and then conference paper four, five, six and I'm just—because I do the research assistant [work] on Monday, Tuesday, any … the time I have to actually prepare the lectures, and the paper is so small. At least it feels that way to me now, so, weekends. I'm not teaching on weekends, that's two days where I can actually just work on it.

Questions of authorship

The issue of acknowledging authorship and contributions to research is important for all academics, and something you must learn to navigate. Many of our interviewees provided stories in which their work, even their substantive writing, was adopted, adapted or used by other researchers without authorship being attributed appropriately. This situation has been acknowledged in the literature. For example, Macfarlane's (2017) survey of academics in Hong Kong found that it was extremely common for research assistants not to be given authorship credit on papers even when they had undertaken a substantial proportion of the work. Our participants agreed that negotiating authorship was often difficult. Kathy worryingly said:

> I don't know if I've been working for ... lousy people, you know? ... because again, it's pitched as, "Well, you've been paid so we can't put your name on it", which I don't get that at all, it doesn't jibe with me, it doesn't make sense to me. Why would that be a thing?

All researchers who have made an intellectual and substantive contribution to a paper should be recognised for their work. There are clearly defined standards for the attribution of authorship, as we will discuss below, but having clear discussions with ethical colleagues is important. As many of our researchers said, working with supervisors and mentors who valued their contributions and invited them to join writing teams as part of their research helped them generate ongoing work, and build a healthy self-concept.

Being named as an author on publications is critical to building an academic portfolio and the order of authorship can be a consideration. Authors in the social sciences and humanities are generally listed in an order that reflects the work undertaken by each contributor with first-named authors having taken the greatest responsibility for the work. According to the widely adopted recommendations put forth by the International Committee of Medical Journal Editors (ICMJE), authorship should be based on meeting at least three of the following criteria:

1 Substantial contributions to the conception or design of the work; or the acquisition, analysis, or interpretation of data for the work; AND
2 Drafting the work or revising it critically for important intellectual content; AND
3 Final approval of the version to be published; AND
4 Agreement to be accountable for all aspects of the work in ensuring that questions related to the accuracy or integrity of any part of the work are appropriately investigated and resolved.

(see www.icmje.org/recommendations/browse/roles-and-responsibilities/defining-the-role-of-authors-and-contributors.html).

While there are many conventions that dictate how authorship should be decided—it is important that you discuss the conventions for any publication you contribute to early, before the emotional labour of the work results in discussions being more delicate.

Many researchers we talked to indicated that their paid work often enabled them to contribute to papers in ways that met some but not all of these criteria. For example, while they may collect and analyse data; and write sections of a paper, they may not be invited to approve the final version or take accountability for the work. Kathy described another project she had worked on:

> I'm submitting [a job] application now and they want to know about my publications. I was actually on a year-long project in 2017 and I was hired—not only was I on the project as a research assistant—but I was hired as an editor on the side. So I sat down and I edited kind of conceptually as well as doing the sort of nuts and bolts—"t-crossing" and "i-dotting" once it had gone through all the conceptual editing side of things. And I received a thanks ... but no, I'm not, I don't get on publications.

This story highlights the complexity that precarious workers may face. Kathy was working more than full-time hours (as a research assistant and editor 'on-the-side'). In her RA role, she had been part of data collection and analysis; in her role as editor she had drafted and revised the manuscript. Yet, she was still left with no publication credit from the project. A key question for contract researchers—and for the academy—is how publication is possible if authorship conventions either are not followed, or not possible within employment expectations. As described above, sometimes contracts will have ended, meaning researchers have moved on to new projects, and may not be given the opportunity to approve final versions, or work on revisions that come back from journals.

The tools for determining authorship are only useful where all members of the project team are willing to commit to applying their logic, even if it means that one or more members of the team might not be named as an author. Some researchers have time built into their contracts to undertake writing, with an expectation of authorship using typical conventions. As Riley said, 'Part of my role is to write and so anything that I contribute to I will be an author on'. Consensus around what constitutes a 'substantive contribution' is often problematic. Time spent mapping out the argument and analysing data may be less visible than the number of words contributed to the final product. The American Mathematical Society (2004) prefers an alphabetised system of authorship known as the *Hardy-Littlewood Rule*, because 'determining which person contributed which ideas is often meaningless because the ideas grow from complex discussions among all partners'. Sarsons's (2017) analysis examines whether co-authored papers using the alphabetised system points to underlying gender discrimination. Examining the trajectories of authors who have published using this convention, Sarson found that an additional co-authored paper was correlated with an 8% increase in tenure for men, as opposed to only 2% for women.

This is where the process of authorship attribution can be fraught. Everyone wants their contribution recognised, and everyone must understand their responsibilities. A first-named author, for example, would normally be expected to undertake a significant portion of the work, and take the lead on managing the paper through to publication. Unfortunately, situations such as this can still arise:

> I was, when I originally started I was supposed to be first author on a lot of those papers, and because ... the second CI, has taken a lot of

them away, I'm guessing I won't be. I'll still be an author, I would have to be at least second author because I did all the work. I did all the interviewing, I did all the focus groups, I did all the analysis of the ... I did everything. So I would still be an author but I might not be first on a few of them.

—Ashley

Initiating publications in a team

Depending on employment contracts and the stage of career, many researchers we spoke to were given the opportunity to contribute to or lead research papers that drew on their own perspectives of research data. A number of contract researchers adopted a proactive approach towards leading publications and asked for lead authorship opportunities within projects. However, academic workloads and priorities sometimes made these publications difficult to achieve. Emma described a situation where she took responsibility as first author and spent a great deal of time writing and leading a journal publication. After unsuccessful attempts at engaging her supervisor and co-author in contributing to her drafts, Emma decided to email it to him and await his input. Months later—on receiving an automated email announcing Emma's decision to leave academia—the co-author made contact about the paper:

so he emailed me and said (imitates friendly tone) "Emma, how are you?" [Laughter] "how's the paper going?" [Laughter]. Yep. And in fact

> it was in *his* lap. He is the one who is on the next draft. He had forgotten that. He thinks I owe him something. I don't. It's his. You know, he's got the next step. But he's so overworked … I might get some authorship, but way down a list somewhere.

However, for many others, the politics and power structures involved in initiating and negotiating ideas for papers, working out collaborations, and the ever-fraught question of authorship were a source of ongoing tension. Ashley said:

> So with initiating publications I've kind of stopped at this point, I kind of just gave up a little bit. I'm just letting the CI run it, because he's kind of he's taken so many potential papers off of me that I've developed, to do it himself, that I've just kind of … I was like well, I'm just going to stop focus. I've just gotten to the point with this particular project that I'm quite apathetic and it's a shame, because I really liked it.

This experience mirrored that of others who had made attempts to take the lead on the development of publications, only to find that the demands of overworked and sometimes unethical academics did not ultimately lead them to publication. The message that many researchers had was to be cognisant of the realities of academic workloads and what this might mean for you; and, wherever possible, to prioritise working with ethical colleagues.

The collective work of career building

Creating and maintaining your networks

Perhaps even more than some other career paths, developing and maintaining strong networks of potential employers is an essential part of being a contract researcher. In this section, we consider the kinds of networks that exist in research contexts—both formal and informal. For example, getting to know other contract researchers, potential employers and academic staff within universities is the primary way of accessing research work, and being able to evaluate which contracts to agree to, and which to avoid. Unfortunately, many contract researchers can feel 'shut out' of formal institutional networks and knowledge. Ashley said:

> We've got the early career researcher development thing that they do for us, and every time I go I get frustrated because it's always every single thing has been based on the idea that you have permanent employment, so all of the help that they give you, all of the strategies to getting grants, or it's to teach better, all that kind of stuff, it's always from someone on continuing, and so whenever you bring up the question of, well how do I "x" if I'm a contract, and then they just don't know how to help you.

Similarly, Heather said:

> I don't know how the research office works at my university. I don't know what the process is for coming up with your own ideas and getting grants.

For this reason, informal networks that researchers establish are vital for progressing as a contract researcher. Because many institutions do not have formal systems in place for helping people progress or maintain viable careers, it is largely up to you to make that happen. Vanessa said:

> I suppose maybe just having some informal networks of contract researchers might be useful, so you can meet up with other people who are in similar positions, and talk about … like, learn from their experiences, and share your own experiences. You might kind of find some opportunities for your next job through that, as well. Or even just how they've managed to, I don't know, just deal with it, really; and you can get some strategies for yourself.

A working paper published for the European Union (Herschberg et al. 2015, p. 25) describes that, in many countries, research assistant positions are allocated based on having personal experience with a professor. In describing post-doctoral positions in Italy, the report indicates that 'although … [recruitment] announcements are public by law, there are often no more than one or two candidates, and they are frequently already known to the supervisor'. As one of the interviewees in the research said, while there is an official procedure, it is often 'rather fictitious' (Herschberg et al. 2015, p. 25). Thus, even when jobs are advertised, personal connections are still important. In Switzerland, for example, although positions are advertised, 'informal discussions between the professors hiring their doctoral students—whom often had already met at Master's level—and postdocs, bringing the candidate to be hired, are frequent' (Fumasoli & Goastellec 2015, p. 83).

The researchers we talked with similarly described the importance of establishing networks of potential employers. Penny, who has been working on contracts for more than a decade in New Zealand and Australia said:

> They hire from within. I've never applied for a job because there's no point. They ... are word-of-mouth.

For a vast number of researchers, these networks stem from their research degree supervisors. Supervisors are often influential in hiring and helping to build networks for early career researchers. Emma, who completed her PhD more than a decade ago, said:

> So I got a little bit [of research work] from my supervisor ... After I finished my PhD I picked up a bit more. Then I was working for another [academic] in a different faculty ... actually I did two projects for her. It was a different area to my PhD but it was fascinating! And also I did some research work in global peace studies. It was quite unrelated. I've since done a little bit of research work in relation to my own [PhD research]. Again with my [former PhD] supervisor ... [Another] guy came through my supervisor. My supervisor is a big expert in my field. So, [that guy] actually contacted my

> supervisor, and then my supervisor contacted me. So, that's really good. And that was nicely paid work ...

Often this work started as small contracts, and gradually grew as researchers built their skills and expertise. In many countries, there is an expectation that researchers should be mobile in order to build their skills and expertise with researchers in specific areas. For example, Penny, who was working in Australia, noted the significant differences in how researchers were employed:

> Yep. And other people realise, okay, you've worked in this, or whatever. Oh great, I need someone with your skills, can you come over and work on this with us. There just does not seem to be the collaboration here. Just doesn't seem to be. It's like I'm protecting my own.
>
> A different thing I found. In New Zealand, we don't necessarily stay where we do our PhD. Here, they stay ... whereas North America, New Zealand, we go [to different universities]. We train you up to go, whereas [in Australia], they just seem to want to [stay at the same university or city/town].

Mendick (2014) indicates that mobility is a form of capital for the middle class. The expectation that researchers can move between institutions, cities, or even countries to build their careers places significant pressure on individuals, and might be limiting for those with relationships, families, specific health needs, community connections, or just those who do not want to leave their home. Yolanda described mobility as having a set of privileges:

I actually think contract work really only benefits those who have certain sets of privileges, so they might not have a family, they can move around and it's not a problem, they might not have any health issues that require access to a particular kind of health service, they may not have issues relating to their gender or sexuality, and so they can live anywhere and they're not going to be discriminated against, same with ethnicity or race or religion. Disability issues, chronic illnesses. I do think contract work only really benefits someone who doesn't have a lot of that in place. And the rest of us we have to try and manage all of those things while staying employed. Because that's the thing academia is like where you need to be willing to move anywhere for work.

Sustaining your network

The importance of sustaining networks of potential employing academics can mean that moving universities (or faculties or countries) is so challenging that many contract researchers choose to remain in the same university or city where possible. Emma said:

That is the other thing that happens. You get stuck doing this sort of contract work. Because you can't leave where you know people.

Broadening your connections beyond your supervisory team or employers is essential, for example because the nature of grants means your supervisor might not always be in a position to offer employment opportunities. As Penny said, being offered a job was:

> very much individuals making decisions about, "Oh, I need someone!" And ... if you don't have those networks, you don't have access to [research work]. I don't have any networks [anymore]. At all three of the universities I've worked at in this city. I've worked with researchers, but they're not named researchers. That just little bits here and there ... They don't have the access to those big grants. Before that, there was research ... but then they all retired. One professor put me onto a major research evaluation project—which was great, but he retired. And with other professors I've worked with having retired too ... so all the people I've worked for ... do I scare them off or something?

A reality for all researchers is that even permanent academics (and universities) who are very happy with your work will not always be in a position to offer work when contracts end. Rebecca said:

> Then I finished my second three-year contract and then the financial situation at [University] was pretty tight and there was not much happening so I was looking elsewhere.

This reality means researchers need to take (and create) opportunities to get to know other academics from their own institutions and beyond. This can be a challenge given the nature of academic work, and sense of wanting to avoid 'stalking' academic staff. Charles said that:

> Well the other thing is, you don't see anybody else because the corridors are empty these days.

For some, being a quiet person made networking a challenge. However, learning to make connections with others was an essential part of finding new contract opportunities.

> I have historically been quite a shy person. I have had to train myself out of that. And in this role, I can't be shy.

For others, the often-solitary nature of research meant that often it was difficult to find new people to connect with.

> [Academics] do often stay in the offices and close the door. And a lot of academics work from home. They don't come in. So, they are often just not people there to talk to. That makes it so hard to get to know people.

The intensification of work for both academic and research staff means that it can be very challenging to find opportunities for face-to-face conversations. As Vanessa said:

> Yeah, that's very isolating, and you want to produce good work, but you can't just stop by and have a chat. You might only see that person once every few months, because they're so busy, if they're a professor or something.

Sustaining and building networks can be time-consuming, which itself can present issues for those whose work is measured on a daily or hourly basis. Attending events such as conferences, research presentations and faculty events is sometimes a useful strategy for getting to know academic staff away from the pressures of the campus. A challenge for many contract researchers, however, is that this work is often not built into employment contracts, which means either negotiating with your employer, or finishing your paid employment outside of these events. David:

> Yeah, so when I've been working for other grants, like at [University], that was on a linkage grant, and that's because ARC doesn't really fund travel. That's the first thing that gets kicked out of a grant if it's funded. So it's just not there.

Describing her working week as split across a university, a hospital and a research centre, Rachel said that:

> I'm spread across so many different areas I do find it hard to participate in any of these social or networking type things. I am a little bit quiet anyway, but I just find that it is quite difficult to find the time, because I'm only in a place you know, one or two days a week … if I go and chat regularly … chat to people for hours and hours during the day, it's going to make very long days for me. So … I mean certainly I know a lot of people, and I like chatting to the people I know, but sadly there's just not enough … not a lot of time for it.

For some researchers, there are pivotal moments in their careers where the research networks they have established are lost, often for reasons outside of the control of the researcher. For example, supervisors and colleagues moving universities or retiring; the death of mentors and supervisors; research departments being closed and so on. When contracts are not extended, for any reason, researchers can lose critical networks that had previously been vital in finding ongoing work. Mark said that:

> you could actually approach people ... I just don't think you can now, well I can't because I just don't know the people.

Mark went on to talk about stories he had heard of contract researchers considering joining churches or community groups (such as Scrabble clubs!) as a means of getting to know academics in a social setting. He concluded that:

> You don't want to know people like that. You know, all these ideas go through your mind about how can I actually go out and meet these people without looking like I was stalking them? But there's no solution really, it's just a matter of, it's luck.

Emma agreed that 'historically academics had time for things ... even just things like morning tea! You know they don't anymore'. Growing numbers of universities, with the privately financed investment into new buildings and campus expansion have been accused of creating 'soulless universities' where increasing numbers of staff work from home, which serves to '[crush] community spirit' (Marriott 2019).

Nevertheless, being proactive and taking any opportunity to get to know others is vital to sustain your networks. For example, if you know a mentor or supervisor is considering retirement, it is a good idea to talk to them (where possible) about how you might start to establish connections with new potential employers and mentors. As Laura's experience (Vignette 3.2) demonstrates, it can be difficult to rebuild these networks when you change institutions. Given the time it takes to establish strong networks, it is also worthwhile trying to make some connections with others as early as possible.

Once you have established a connection with a more senior academic, seeking some kind of mentoring—often on an informal basis—can be helpful. Some universities offer mentoring programs, which may be a useful way of making new connections with more senior researchers, as Rachel explained:

> So, 2005 I started. And another thing that helped with me getting into research as well was my university had a mentor program [in the Honors year] … I got placed with someone at a hospital who was working on researching early psychosis, and I got a bit of work through them at the beginning.

Vignette 3.2: Laura's experience of rebuilding networks

Laura has worked as a researcher for more than a decade. She has had multiple moments in her career that her networks collapsed. She began her research career by working for her two doctoral supervisors, who unfortunately both left her institution shortly after her PhD. She explained the importance of losing these mentors early in her research career. Despite being a well-regarded scholar in his field, one of her supervisors left because he felt he was in an untenable and unstable employment situation himself. Laura reflected that:

> So the university lost someone that had this incredible wealth of knowledge and experience and he's now a deputy director at an institute at a university in another state. But he was just being kept as a sessional lecturer … and he just couldn't stand it. He had three children and a partner and … you know.

Laura's second supervisor decided to leave academia altogether. Watching this situation unfold was difficult, as it demonstrated from early on the nature of employment in universities:

> they were both amazing people because of their incredible skills and commitment to teaching and learning. And they were just doing everything else on top of that—research, coordinating programs, writing courses. They just worked around the clock. And then were not valued or rewarded for it … And it's hard as a student to watch that happen and to know … it's not really something to

> aim for is it? But then they left, and it was like, I no longer really know anyone in the institution.

This situation meant that Laura needed to re-establish her networks quickly:

> Because you need those networks early on in your career … if they leave it's so hard to re-establish … I think that's what happened to me. Anyone who could have networked me in [after my PhD] was gone.

Laura worked hard to establish new contacts, eventually finding work in a specialist research centre that was jointly funded by government and her (PhD) university. She spent the next four years at the centre, but as she described it, her employment would depend 'on what bucket of money they could dip into', which meant that she was either employed casually or on three or six-month long contracts.

> Interviewer: Even though you were virtually doing the same job [for four years]?
> Laura: Oh nothing changed! Nothing changed!

While this position provided work for four years, the downside of the role was that it was geographically located away from the university campus, so it isolated Laura from academic staff, and meant she had almost no contacts when a change of government led to the research centre being closed. Once again, Laura was in the position of asking colleagues about possible work and seeking to re-establish new networks. At the time of her interview, Laura worked across a number of universities, on a range of research projects. She reflected that:

> When I see people doing their PhD, I almost see someone who's networked in, because they have a supervisor. And I think that's something I lost a long time ago. So I think all of these years have just been off me getting jobs. Making my own networks.

Conferences and professional organisations

A number of researchers talked about conferences as an opportunity to meet and talk with other researchers and potential employers. Attending conferences may not lead to immediate opportunities, but can be a longer-term strategy for broadening your networks:

> Conferences are a way for you to meet people. Conferences are where opportunities happen … and when I'm talking about opportunities, I'm not even talking about real jobs… possibly, maybe if you get lucky, sometime down the road … I actually went purposefully and spoke to a key person here. Introduced myself at the

> conference, said, "This is me, this is who I am, I'm looking for work" and then followed up with emails and stuff until they gave me a job.
>
> —Emma

Where possible, it is worthwhile being strategic about which conferences you might attend. Where will you have opportunities to talk with people in your field, to build and maintain your contacts? It is also worth strengthening contacts with people you meet at conferences through emails after the conference to discuss possible collaborations.

Conferences are also a good opportunity to develop new skills and knowledge, and to expand your CV. Donna reflected that:

> Like, you know ... I went to [a conference] in New York this year and that's fantastic, I don't underestimate the opportunity or ... I really value and very thankful and grateful for the opportunities I get in my role ... and I think that's wonderful ... I get to learn every day and I get to improve my skills ...

However, the reality for many researchers is that conference registration and accommodation pose a significant financial burden for researchers. David, along with many others said that self-funding, especially without the security of ongoing work was a major financial decision.

> The membership is so high for somebody on my salary. If you are a student, then there is a nice discount but if you are making money, they assume that you are making that all the

time. That is the other challenge. I am always thinking about that precarious situation. They have great stuff for students but they aren't thinking about the adjuncts and contract researchers, who have to go to present their own stuff.

Joining professional and research organisations and attending conferences and events can be expensive. While some organisations offer tiered funding for students, it is rare that lower registration rates are available for researchers on part-time or precarious contracts. Ashley said:

you have to pay for it yourself, and I just think they don't really account for people like me in precarious situations … if my contract doesn't get renewed at the end of the year I would be going from a really decent salary to nothing.

Supportive employers can assist contract researchers with professional development opportunities and assist with securing funding for conference through research funding or institutional support.

Networks of contract researchers

You really need … you've really got … I don't have any positions right now that were advertised and you just have to constantly think about, am I sellable, am I employable? Because we're so spread out and we're not unified and you never see the other casual

> academics, I don't know what competition is out there. I don't know who I'm up against.
> —David

There is a temptation for contract researchers to see each other as potential competition. We do not dispute that this might be the case, given the limited pool of funds and jobs available. However, the researchers we talked to found their ability to find and sustain work with ethical and kind supervisors to be greatly enhanced by adopting a collegial approach to others.

Strong networks enable contract researchers to be more selective in taking on work and choosing to work for employers who take an ethical stance. Rachel, who has worked on contract for over a decade said having supportive networks of other researchers was essential for self-preservation. Having worked in various institutions (universities, research institutes, hospitals) including on a number of projects where she felt bullied, Rachel's networks helped her to find out more about employers she hadn't worked for, including their ethical and personal approaches when working with researchers. She said:

> For jobs for the most part, I try and find out about the people that I'm going to work for, if I don't know them ... I ask people ... that [have] worked for them. Because some of these people [who employ you], they can be very nice when you're not working for them, but as soon as they're your manager they can become really difficult to work with. And like I said, I honestly do think some of these people do genuinely have things wrong with them, yeah. So I will always ask, try and find out about that person.

Rachel acknowledged that her experience meant she had many other peers to ask about their prior experiences but felt that even new researchers should 'ask around' and find out more about the experiences of others before accepting contracts. Rachel's experience had taught her that power imbalances between project leads and precariously employed researchers could result in bullying and have a significant impact on wellbeing. Now working full-time and happily employed across two different universities and a hospital, Rachel reflected on a project some years earlier:

> One where I'd probably rather have jumped in front of a bus than get on it to come to work. Terrible. Yeah, yeah. It's horrible. I can remember catching the bus to work some days thinking "Gee, I wish we'd crash".

This experience led to Rachel feeling it was essential to ask other researchers about lead investigators because it was often difficult to assess what it would be like to work on a project based on personal knowledge:

> Yeah, there are some people that might've had quite a good reputation but they turn out to be quite disappointing to work for or work with. Which is a real shame, because there are some jobs that I've had that could've been really great opportunities that were just squandered by the team being very poorly run.

Being able to trust your peers by sharing your knowledge and experiences is an important way of seeking out employers who will respect you as a researcher. We note, however, that some of our participants pointed out that gossiping or complaining is unprofessional.

Networks can not only provide future employment opportunities but also offer the exchange of what is often largely tacit knowledge about 'how things work': how to draw on social support to combat anxiety and imposter syndrome; learning through shared experience; offering and receiving 'in kind' support. These supports are invaluable for contract researchers.

Collectivisation among researchers

We shift from a more individual perspective on networks to considering how networks of contract researchers may engage in collective action to engage with the institution and senior academics to have their needs met, in ways that could, as acknowledged in Chapter 2, present challenges for individuals.

Although institutional principles and policies do exist for the greater inclusion of contract researchers, there is often a distinct mismatch between the spirit of such policies and their realisation in practice. This is in part a critique of universities and other research organisations, but also a critique of the broader structures according to which it 'makes sense' for the research workforce to maintain its current organisation. These structures undermine the core purpose of research in higher education and beyond, and we conclude our account with a look back at our opening chapter, the political and economic conditions which have led us to this situation, and take a prospective look at possible ways in which better alternatives might be realised.

We offer below a vignette of a researcher development group, which we use in part to illustrate the great potential of collective researcher activities—as well as offering concrete examples of these activities in action. This account demonstrates the affordances and potential limits of collective activities.

> ### Vignette 3.3: *Fairweather* Researcher Group—an example of researcher collaborative practice
>
> *A brief history of the group*
>
> Based in a UK university, *Fairweather* came about in 2015 through an interdisciplinary Research Centre that was funded by a grant that included a stated commitment to supporting researcher experience and development. When the bid was successful, the centre director approached five researchers, a mixture of old and new, and asked them to put together a concrete proposal for what this researcher support and development might look like. One researcher had this work included in her role. In 2015–16, a number of newly recruited researchers joined the centre, generating a sense of a community and 'critical mass' out of which *Fairweather* was formed. Six months later a Research Fellow was recruited to the Centre who had facilitation and development of *Fairweather* included in her role—therefore providing funded resource to support the endeavour.
>
> Researchers were invited to join a weekly writing group, providing the team with a reason to meet regularly. The initial proposal for *Fairweather*

emerged from these discussions, and focused on four broad themes:

1 Writing and publishing;
2 Grant funding;
3 Career and contract support; and
4 Peer-support.

Over the first 12 months, *Fairweather* grew from six or seven core members to around 50 members located in a variety of different schools and faculties.
Some examples of core activities were:

Writing and publishing activities

- 'Shut up and write' sessions[1] were established as a collective writing activity. *Fairweather* created a weekly time and PIs and line managers were asked to support the groups informally by 'releasing' researchers from project demands. The sessions became an important part of the collective work and identity of the group.
- *'Paper development workshops'* were organised every six months, for which researchers submitted works in progress to be reviewed by their peers and senior academics and discussed as a group. *At least one professor participated in every group.* Participants submitted a clear plan for the forward development of the paper and track their targets.

Grant funding activities

- *A funding mailing list* was established. This researcher-only mailing list shared information about upcoming opportunities and invited informal discussions to increase the involvement of contract researchers in grants led by senior academics and encourage more researcher-led grants. Although there was some success, there were also instances of grant applications characterised by a lack of openness and transparency about who would be involved.

Career and contract activities

- *Contract and project tracker.* Essentially a spreadsheet for the Research Centre to track researcher contract end dates alongside upcoming project start dates and funding application windows. The purpose of this tool was to improve the centre's ability to match people to projects more proactively and systematically. A dedicated bridging fund was made available that could be applied to in the event that a researcher nearing the end of a contract might be kept in post if there was upcoming grant money to support them within three months.

  A good idea in principle, this tool needed to be carefully managed and monitored. Explicit support was required from HR to ensure there was no conflict with employment policies (e.g. redeployment policies). A limit to the success of this initiative was the lack of openness and transparency in how employment decisions were made.

Peer-support and networking

The Centre had a regular program of invited external speakers and *Fairweather* negotiated additional time for researcher development activities with each speaker. This took several different forms—for example:

- Dedicated one-to-one sessions with researchers to discuss draft papers
- Sessions from journal editors to explain the scope and editing processes of particular journals
- Q&A sessions about career development run by established academics.

The most generous support often came from visiting international scholars who were able to provide multiple sessions spread over several days.

The limits of success

The practical examples above offer some insight into the achievements of the Centre, while also indicating some of the challenges encountered. The Research Centre flourished, partly due to the considerable success of *Fairweather* and proposed to become a permanent Institute, asking *Fairweather* to contribute to the proposal, requiring the group to evaluate their practices and propose ways in which this success could be extended.

The first objective was achieved by asking all members to track publication progress and quantify the impact that the writing-focused activities had. This was sometimes difficult because researchers were understandably concerned about how this data might be used and wanted assurances that it would not become part of formal performance reviews. As such, an anonymised spreadsheet was developed by core members of *Fairweather*. This is an instructive example, because it highlights the careful attention that must be paid to both informal and formal processes and the vulnerability of staff. The processes that were instituted meant that writing activities within *Fairweather* were evaluated demonstrating *around four or five times the number of journal submissions made by researchers 'before' and 'after'* Fairweather's *establishment.*

The second core objective was to propose options for building on the success of the group by being part of a wider institute with the goal of becoming a sustainable centre that focused on better supporting, including and developing researchers. While some suggestions were taken into consideration, many could not be, because of broader structural barriers such as research funding mechanisms and university HR policies. For example, in response to a suggestion of introducing a minimum standard length of contract, the director noted that 'It is not possible to underwrite researcher contracts beyond that for which there is demonstrable income'.

Becoming an institute and the attempted formalisation of the network

After the establishment of the Institute, *Fairweather* was seen as a critical element of its raison d'être. However, a number of the original members of *Fairweather* had left at the end of their contracts to take up new roles and some of the Centre board members also moved on to new roles. During this period informal researcher collective action and formal *Fairweather* activity declined and *Fairweather*

> became in essence mainly a contract researcher mailing list rather than a researcher-led set of activities.
>
> In 2019, a meeting was convened by the Institute directors for researchers to establish a new strategy for *Fairweather*. There was little enthusiasm for volunteering for roles to continue the research collective leaving *Fairweather* to now exist in name only.

Fairweather's history demonstrates the great potential that can be generated through collective, researcher-led activities. It also demonstrates a tension between formal and informal structures and activities, which goes to the heart of the problem of *making it* as a contract researcher. *Making it* requires the mobilisation of significant (and often unpaid) effort on the part of researchers, the majority of which might be 'invisible work' (Smith 1987). The core tension then is that *making it* as a contract researcher, means much more than just obtaining a contract. A multitude of the activities that are central to *making it* are conducted under-the-radar. Ultimately, this means that work researchers put into their collective support and development must find a means of connecting with formal organisational policies and practices, so as to become more enduring.

A final word

Researcher collectivisation may not always be expected given the project-basis of research—talking to others who work on disparate projects may not seem to be a good use of time. However, the rise of insecure work has reduced the bargaining power and collective entitlements of individual researchers. Working together is a dominant strategy used by many researchers to maintain their networks, and to protect their financial and mental health. In Chapter 4 we move to discuss the broader structural issues that govern the everyday world of contract researchers.

Note

1 https://thesiswhisperer.com/shut-up-and-write/

References

Allen-Collinson, J. & Hockey, J., 1998, 'Capturing contracts: Informal activity among contract researchers', *British Journal of Sociology of Education*, vol. 19, no. 4, pp. 497–515.

American Mathematical Society, 2004, *The Culture of Research and Scholarship in Mathematics: Joint Research and Its Publication*, www.ams.org/profession/leaders/culture/CultureStatement04.pdf, accessed 4 July 2019.

Broadbent, K. & Strachan, G., 2016, '"It's difficult to forecast your longer term career milestone": Career development and insecure employment for research academics in Australian universities", *Labour & Industry: A Journal of the Social and Economic Relations of Work*, vol. 26, no. 4, pp. 251–265, doi: 10.1080/10301763.2016.1243438.

Bryson, C. & Barnes, N., 2000, 'The casualisation of employment in Higher Education in the United Kingdom', in M Tight (ed), *Academic Work and Life and How This Is Changing*, West Yorkshire, UK: Emerald Insight. pp. 187–241.

Deuchar, R., 2008, 'Facilitator, director or critical friend? Contradiction and congruence in doctoral supervision styles', *Teaching in Higher Education*, vol. 13, no. 4, pp. 489–500.

Fumasoli, T. & Goastellec, G., 2015, 'Global models, disciplinary and local patterns in academic recruitment processes', in T. Fumasoli;

G. Goastellec and B. Kehm (eds), *Academic Work and Careers in Europe: Trends, challenges, Perspectives*, Cham: Springer. pp. 69–93.

Gill, R., 2010, 'Breaking the silence: The hidden injuries of neo-liberal academia', in R Flood and R Gill (eds), *Secrecy and Silence in the Research Process: Feminist Reflections*, London: Routledge, pp. 228–244.

Green, A.E. & Turok, I., 2000, 'Employability, adaptability and flexibility: Changing labour market prospects', *Regional Studies*, vol. 34, no. 7, pp. 599–600.

Harney, B., Monks, K., Alexopoulos, A., Buckley, F. & Hogan, T., 2014, 'University research scientists as knowledge workers: Contract status and employment opportunities', *International Journal of Human Resource Management*, vol. 25, no. 16, pp. 2219–2233, doi: 10.1080/09585192. 2011.561241.

Herschberg, C., Benschop, Y.W.M. & van den Brink, M.C.L., 2015, *Constructing Excellence: The Gap between Formal and Actual Selection Criteria for Early Career Academics*, Trento, IT: University of Trento.

Hey, V., 2001, 'The construction of academic time: Sub/Contracting academic labour in research', *Journal of Education Policy*, vol. 16, no. 1, pp. 67–84, doi: 10.1080/02680930010009831.

Knights, D. & Clarke, C.A., 2014, 'It's a bittersweet symphony, this life: Fragile academic selves and insecure identities at work', *Organization Studies*, vol. 35, no. 3, pp. 335–357.

Loveday, V., 2018, 'The neurotic academic: Anxiety, casualisation, and governance in the neoliberalising university', *Journal of Cultural Economy*, vol. 11, no. 2, pp. 154–166.

Marriott, J., 2019, 'Soulless universities eat away at mental health', *The Times*, 6 June www.thetimes.co.uk/article/soulless-universities-eat-away-at-mental-health-mx2km5jqt, accessed 14 July 2019.

McCulloch, S., 2017, *Negotiating the Associate Researcher Role*, https://patthomson.net/2017/03/22/negotiating-the-associate-researcher-role/, accessed 4 July 2019.

Macfarlane, B., 2017, 'The ethics of multiple authorship: Power, performativity and the gift economy', *Studies in Higher Education*, vol. 42, no. 7, pp. 1194–1210, doi: 10.1080/03075079.2015.1085009.

Mendick, H., 2014, 'Social class, gender and the pace of academic life: What kind of solution is slow?', *Forum Qualitative Sozialforschung/ Forum: Qualitative Social Research*, vol. 15, no. 3.

Park, C., 2007, 'New variant PhD: The changing nature of the doctorate in the UK', *Journal of Higher Education Policy and Management*, vol. 27, no. 5, pp. 189–207.

Sarsons, H., 2017, 'Recognition for group work: Gender differences in academia', *American Economic Review*, vol. 107, no. 5, pp. 141–145.

Smith, D.E., 1987, *The Everyday World as Problematic: A Feminist Sociology*. Toronto: University of Toronto Press.

Thomson, P., 2017, 'A researcher on someone else's project?', *Patter*, https://patthomson.net/2017/03/06/a-researcher-on-someone-elses-project/, accessed 30 August 2019.

Wilson, M. & Holligan, C., 2013, 'Performativity, work-related emotions and collective research identities in UK university education departments: An exploratory study', *Cambridge Journal of Education*, vol. 43, no. 2, pp. 223–241.

4 The possible future of research careers

Nurturing engagement

One way universities can support staff taking their first steps into research is by providing information. An easily accessible webpage where academics can peruse previous successful (and unsuccessful) research bids, ethics applications, chapter proposals and such like would enable early career researchers to see what the standards are, to use successful examples as models and to develop an understanding of what they are aiming for. I always share these things if people ask and I urge you to do the same, but they shouldn't really have to ask. There should be a system.

One of the most valuable things universities can do to support their staff is to run a mentoring system or support group for early career researchers. This can give early career researchers the space to talk about their ideas, to ask questions, to share concerns and to feel that they're not alone. More experienced researchers, whether in the role of mentor or not, could act as critical friends to their colleagues, reading drafts, sharing calls for papers and leading on collaborative projects. This should, of course, be included in workload models.

Line managers can ensure that wider developmental goals are written into personal development plans without being linked to promotion or evaluative regimes like the REF.[1] Taking modest steps into research without too much pressure can nurture job satisfaction and wellbeing. Managers can also take an interest; if someone in the team presented a paper, ask how it went. Taking an interest shows that research is valued and contributes to creating a supportive, research-oriented environment.

These steps might not lead directly to four-star outputs, but we have to be realistic. We could all benefit from a bit less attention to rankings and metrics and a bit more focus on nurturing engagement with research at a level that is meaningful and achievable for all of us, not just the high fliers.

—Reflections of a contract researcher

Supporting contract researchers to *make it*

In Chapter 1, we discussed what *making it* might mean for contract researchers in universities or research institutes that are characterised by neoliberal agendas. While we recognise the need for structural changes within universities and research organisations, change of this nature takes time. Resistance to the ever-increasing expectations for quantifiable research outputs and measures of impact have laid some of the foundations for structural change. For current contract researchers, many of these changes (such as the 'slow academic' movement (e.g. Berg & Seeber 2016)) do not address the unique challenges of their work. Sometimes moves to resist the pressures of the modern neoliberal university can be viewed as being at odds with the needs of those who are insecurely employed. Others have written about how efforts by university staff to disrupt neoliberal agendas are only available to those in positions of power (i.e. tenured professors) (*cf* Carrigan & Vostal 2016; Mendick 2014).

What *is* clear is that there is an urgent need for change. As we have described throughout this book, contract researchers face conditions that can pose barriers for career progression and make continued engagement in research work untenable. In this chapter, we discuss how institutions and tenured academics can better support precarious researchers in the current context. We consider structural and policy changes that might redress some of the challenges and barriers they face. Building on previous chapters, we take a look at institutional and government policy and practice, and how these might be translated into enduring systemic change. We believe that potential pathways for change can be broadly grouped into seven categories, as represented in Table 4.1.

While broader problems such as the role of the state (e.g. the allocation of research funding) and the increasing reliance of governments all over the world upon private equity are not things that can be tackled in a book such as this, these seven categories offer a framework for strategies, which can go on *in spite of* the broader changes required in order to bring about some material improvements to the experiences of researchers, *and* to better support the production of quality research.

Table 4.1 Pathways for change

Level of change	Key concerns
Individual	Individual contract researchers seeking fairness in their individual circumstances.
Group	Groups of contract researchers working collaboratively to improve outcomes for all.
Supervisory	Staff (typically tenured academics) who are concerned with supporting the contract researchers they employ on an insecure basis.
Industrial	Workers (both contract and tenured) addressing the issue of insecure employment as an industrial issue, often through participation in trade unions.
Research and professional bodies	Professional bodies and research associations concerned with more equitably representing a wider membership that includes those who are employed insecurely.
Institutional	Universities, research institutes and organisations, concerned with supporting more equitable and sustainable employment and research policies and practices within their own organisations.
Government	Governments and government organisations concerned with ensuring policies, structures and practices do not reproduce structural industrial inequalities in employment (including at the national level).

Individual efforts

As we outlined in Chapter 1, contract researchers frequently seek employment out of economic necessity ahead of disciplinary or organisational fit, meaning it is vital for researchers to be informed about the kinds of job and kinds of institution on offer. Substantial differences between universities/institutes/research groups and individual employers translate into material differences in the experience of employment, opportunities for support and development, and possibilities for future employment. In the absence of wider changes, it is vital that the research workforce enters into this precarious world of work with their eyes open.

We want to stress that contract researchers should not be solely responsible for managing the issues associated with contract work. Focusing the need for resistance against the structural issues inherent within the current system on individual action can place people at risk, of being seen as 'troublesome' or internalising these challenges as their own fault. While we have attempted to provide practical ideas for individuals in Chapters 2 and 3, we also hope that the discussion supports more open conversations about conditions of work at all levels within and beyond research institutions.

Group work: collectivisation among researchers

In Chapter 3, we discussed the importance of collegiality, collaboration and collectivisation. The self-organised character of researcher support and development is both a problem and an opportunity—in the words of

Raewyn Connell, in her interview; 'don't agonise, organise!' The isolation inherent in a lot of research work, particularly throughout doctoral study, can make it difficult for researchers to build knowledge about appropriate conditions and expectations in research careers. A number of contract researchers we talked to had gaps in their knowledge that led them to question the viability of their career paths: a lack of access to knowledge about funding regulations, conference support, leave entitlements and workplace supports can stem from the isolation that is frequently part of contract research.

We have alluded at several points to the problematic lack of visibility of contract researchers, who are less conspicuous than academic teaching staff. There is a widespread lack of awareness especially among tenured academic (and non-academic) staff of the conditions under which contract researchers are labouring. In conversation with contract researcher colleagues, Zara described the period of time when a redundancy scheme affected permanent academic colleagues:

> Annie shared her anger and incredulity that lecturers, in their outrage about potential involuntary redundancies, were being so insensitive in their school-wide email missives. She said that this was not because it was not a worrying time for them, but because they did so with a lack of care about who they included or how they framed their messages without reference to contract researcher colleagues who are repeatedly made redundant.

Such anecdotes are symptomatic of obliviousness to contract researchers' lived experiences rather than being an indication of any malice towards them. Nonetheless they manifest micro-aggressions that contribute to contract researchers' marginalisation and disconnection from the institution and institutional colleagues and embedding of discrimination (Sue 2010).

Collective activity by contract researchers can help to make contract researchers more visible to more senior academic colleagues and raise awareness of their value as well as their precarious situation. This kind of relational approach involves contract researchers building solidarity with tenured and teaching colleagues and making their voices heard in governance matters, on research committees and other institutional fora. Good practice charters alone will not change the situation—contract researchers need to be seen and heard.

Supervisory action and ethical leadership

One aspect of discussions of casualisation in the academy that receives minimal attention in the research literature is the duty of care or ethical responsibilities of those who employ contract researchers to work on their projects. Our interviews with contract researchers and the research literature demonstrate that supervisors can make a substantial difference in the employment experiences and opportunities available to contract researchers. Archer et al.'s (2018) work in New Zealand similarly demonstrated the significant impact of line managers on employment stress among casual employees. The relationship between managers and contract employees directly impacts on 'the day-to-day workplace treatment casual workers receive, and also on other elements of the broader employment relationship, such as work flexibility, hours of work allocated, income level, certainty of work, facilities provided, and inclusion in social and communication networks' (Archer et al. 2018, p. 14). Supervisors can act as a lifeline to the organisation and can 'insulate' researchers from some of the inequities of the 'greedy' institution (Bone et al. 2018). Many of the positive descriptions in our interviews are attributed to the fact that a number of supervisors have been contract researchers themselves. As Catherine stated:

> I suppose she's just very conscious of my CV, putting me up for committee memberships, and lots of talking about papers and publications, and going to conferences, and meeting other people in the field working on similar stuff, but also different things. I think she found it quite hard, as a contract researcher, so she's [providing] a good experience for me.

Our interviewees overwhelmingly reported higher satisfaction with their work when they felt supported by their supervisors, valued as a member of a research team and like they were contributing to a larger goal. Examples of concrete support such as mentoring, opportunities for publications, conference attendance and potential future funding are appreciated but not taken for granted. Bridget stated:

> When I started I had a Research Fellow line manager who ... sent me to a conference because I'd never been to one before, to see what it was like before I had to present—brilliant for a young and naive RA.

Despite their significant role in supporting and developing future researchers, supervision of contract academic work is a task for which there is little, if any, preparation or training and support, and is rarely acknowledged as a responsibility (Ryan et al. 2013). A major report into the management of Australian contract academics found 'virtually no instances of formalised standards of practice or professional development for the subject coordinator' to manage casual academics (Percy et al. 2008, p. 13). This is a notable disparity from new lecturers who are often given formal supervisory support and development. As Helen Sword noted when we talked with her:

> There are so many ways in which researchers in general could be so much better supported, you know, my own university there's, and it's the case most places I think, there's very little, I think we're, with researcher development where we were with teaching development about 30 years ago, you know, sort of internationally, so there's an expectation for everyone, publish or perish, including even to get the PhD, much less what you do after that ... it's assumed that you know how to do everything and you don't need any sort of support structure around it, or, if there's a support structure, it's something like, "oh let's make sure that our first year academics have a mentor", without any understanding of what that might mean or how to do that well.

We argue that as people who occupy positions of power, research supervisors have a responsibility to ensure that all of those who they employ are treated fairly and that conditions are put in place to support both effective work and the wellbeing of all researchers. In material terms, this includes providing clear expectations of hours of work, recognising the other responsibilities that researchers have, and, depending on the length of their contract, discussing strategies for support in advance of contract end. This responsibility reflects a need for the ethical leadership of research work.

Developed for school leadership, Starratt (2012, 2014) describes a model of ethical leadership that we argue is equally applicable to research work, comprising three inter-related ethics: *ethics of care, justice and critique*. An *ethic of care*, in this context, is conceived of as developing relationships that respect the rights and individuality of others. Thus, an *ethic of care* promotes the development of open, trusting relationships with contract researchers that 'honors the dignity and integrity of each person' (Starratt 2014, p. 55). Supervisors and line managers need to understand the individual circumstances of the contract researchers in their employ, who need to develop their own career while working on a shared research project.

An *ethic of justice*, in simple terms, relates to the fair distribution of resources among members of the community. When considered in the context of contract research, *an ethic of justice* requires supervisors and lead researchers to ensure that everyone they employ is paid fairly and under conditions that promote equity. A system built on temporary employment, with a scarcity of jobs, and variable and poorly defined career paths offers few structural conditions upon which to pursue such an ethic. Research into the casualisation of academic positions has also uncovered gendered discrimination, suggesting a clear need for recognition of a primarily female workforce and those with caring responsibilities. A fair system of employment provides contract researchers with clearly defined expectations and hours of work and clear policies for leave, compensation, and financial remuneration.

The *ethic of critique* challenges all researchers, particularly those permanently employed within the university setting to adopt a critical stance that questions which groups or individuals are privileged or disadvantaged by current systems. It compels tenured academics to become allies of those in precarious employment to question current structures that create inequity and provide a catalyst to the development of fair and equitable practices. If the situation is going to change, those people employing researchers on short- or fixed-term contracts have a responsibility to actively critique unfair practices and negotiate more reasonable conditions for those in tenuous employment. In order to be effective, such critique must be undertaken collectively, and seek both formal and informal means of leverage, as illustrated by the following excerpt from an article in the *Higher Education Chronicle* entitled 'How to be a generous professor in precarious times':

> One of us witnessed the collective effort of a department to convert a contingent teaching position into a permanent one. The process of building consensus began with two tenured professors who had observed the adjunct's excellent teaching. They proceeded to go door-to-door, meeting with every colleague in the department to gain support for the idea. With everyone on board, the entire department then worked together to deliver a consistent

> message to the administration: "We need this person". In the meantime, the department avoided promising the adjunct that the conversion could actually be accomplished. And when it was, we celebrated it as a victory not just for the individual but for the department.
>
> Generosity may start with a person, but like any radical movement, it slowly builds. It unifies people, and those unified people stand together in a group that grows as the proposal goes up the ladder. At every rung there is the possibility of failure.
>
> (Dowland & Pérez 2018, unpaginated)

Supervisors can act as allies to critique and challenge practices that disadvantage contract researchers. Including those on short- or fixed-term contracts in academic meetings and discussions, collaborating with them about research processes and supporting them to build their own career beyond the individual project can all make an enormous difference to those in precarious positions. Raewyn Connell reflected on her own practice as a supervisor:

> I've always tried to design my practice with a couple of things in mind. One—defining tasks for people I was employing, which gave them a chance to exercise a wide range of skills. So not just as doing interviews, but also designing interviews, constructing samples, interpreting findings, sharing the write-up of findings and so forth. And, in some cases, also taking on a significant part of the management of the project.

> And the second thing I've tried to do is to make the work relevant to their careers in so far as I was able to give some kind of continuity. That's been, that is very difficult for an academic to arrange because this kind of work depends on winning grants ... competitive grant schemes ... which are always fixed-term, and which often don't cover a full salary for the full length of the project, they usually don't. So it's then a question of trying to get more research grants to provide another few years of work to someone so they can build up a portfolio of experience that they can then build on and to give them some kind of continuity of employment.

As described in Chapters 2 and 3, supervisors can have an enormous impact on contract researchers' experiences of their work and career trajectory. Examples of strong supervisory support included encouraging co-authorship and for contract researchers to take the lead on publications; clear and consistent explanations for the expectations of research work; and, helping researchers map out a career path. This approach is not just good for contract researchers, it works to build a mutually supportive research team. We have witnessed clear examples of how researchers who work with ethical leaders feel more included and more productive in these supportive environments. Strong research teams retain researchers, building a critical mass of organisational knowledge and strengthening innovation and performance (Bain et al. 2001). In supporting and mentoring the development of contract researchers, lead researchers can build strong networks of collaborators, who they can work with into the future. In a reflection on her own career, Professor Sue Scott (2019) writes:

> We have all absorbed, to a greater or lesser extent, the culture of individualism over recent decades ... we can't, at the same time, rail against the neo liberal University, and have only individualistic expectations. We need to work across the academic generations, and with middle and senior management, to engender solidarity and make common cause, as well as ensuring that we all have the supportive networks that we need both inside and outside of the University. We, and especially senior academics, need to a think about how to make Universities good places to begin a career ... because if it is then it will be a good place for everyone. This is not simply about being nicer to each other and doing a bit more mentoring, but about having constructively critical conversations and plans. This may sound naïve, even hopeless, but we need to stop talking about 'The University' and blaming them up there and work together to make it 'Our University'. If we don't, we will be cogs in a wheel rather than its designers—time to reinvent it!

The role of those in power, supervisors, line-managers and employers, can make an enormous difference to building positive experiences and the capacity of those who are not tenured. Expanding upon a guest post she wrote for *Patter* (https://patthomson.net/), Teena Clarke (see Vignette 4.1) describes the potential advantages of these relationships and the negative outcomes that can emerge when research leadership is less-than-ideal.

Vignette 4.1: Supervision and support (by Teena Clarke)

At present, I am concurrently working on eight research projects, each with different funding bodies and regulations, budgets, partnerships and research practices. This means I have eight bosses with different expectations of how or whether RA supervision, support and collaboration are part of the deal.

Good fortune landed me early in my research career with two exemplary mentors—the late Alison Lee who was my PhD supervisor, and Nick Hopwood, himself one of Alison's supervisees. One of Alison's passions and areas of expertise was doctoral pedagogy, which she saw as research training. She taught by leading, with generosity, kindness and constructive critique, moving me from student to researcher. Nick led with enthusiasm, care and clear guidelines and expectations, staging tasks to my developing capabilities. Our research collaboration has produced a number of co-authored scholarly and practitioner publications, presentations and workshops.

Without exception, my RA work has come through word of mouth, rather than a formal application process. This means you are as good as your last job. Word gets around if you stuff up. Thus, Chief Investigators (CIs) I have been referred to need to know I am capable, so I take on tasks I have not previously done, which means I learn on the go. While both CI and I are aware I am learning, supervision can vary from complete hands-off, to being given vague tips, to micro management, sometimes after I've spent time trying to figure it out myself. This means I often work twice what I am contracted/paid because it takes me longer and I usually have to do things more than once.

Supervisors can vary greatly in terms of project management capacity, digital filing systems and timeframes. Some say tomorrow and it doesn't matter if it's three weeks, while others say, oh plenty of time and then two days later, email to say they need it by Monday (and it's Friday).

Good RA supervision means CIs and team members are collegial and collaborative, rather than unavailable and/or micro managers. It means processes, resources, and tasks are clearly established and fulfilled, with appropriate guidance or scaffolded support provided for unfamiliar tasks. In such cases, RAs learn more, yet are also able to say what they can or cannot do, and what they need help with. Good supervision also means there is space for RAs to draw on skills and knowledge from previous work, such as project management, research methodologies and writing formats.

For me, poorly supervised projects have left me feeling metaphorically beaten and exploited, inadequate, naïve and dumb. In contrast, well supervised projects have facilitated the expansion of my knowledge across disciplinary domains and topics and the development of my research literacies. I am fortunate to have been entrusted with the stories and experiences of hundreds of people across NSW, Australia, Europe and the UK, which makes a difference in the world. It is not frivolous work.

> At the end of the day, RA work is simultaneously difficult, frustrating, complex, often underpaid and lonely, and immensely rewarding and fun. Poor supervision exacerbates the negatives, while good supervision is like snowballing, enabling an RA to pick up more work, while increasing capabilities.

Industrial action: the role of unions and activism

A number of unions in the higher education space are starting to pay attention to the problem of precarious work. In many cases, however, unions are focused on sessional teaching staff. In the UK, for example the University and College Union (UCU) offers discounted memberships to 'support people at the start of their education careers',[2] which includes several kinds of non-permanent staff, however, UCU's criteria stipulate that individuals must be 'part of the teaching and assessment team' to get the reduced rate, which excludes many contract researchers. This situation must change if contract researchers are to be recognised, and feel their contribution is valued.

The UCU reduced fees initiative is part of a broader campaign, *Stamp out Casualisation*,[3] which opposes increasing levels of temporary employment, and includes a pledge to better support the rights and interests of casualised workers (such as initiating negotiations over greater job security, recruiting casual representatives and setting up local anti-casualisation groups). Nonetheless, the main objectives of the campaign and the majority of its progress to date, relate to the casual employment of teaching staff.

Academic and research staff have also engaged in some activism, developing alternative manifestos for the contemporary university. These alternative manifestos have been situated in the context of a series of high-profile restructuring programmes in several UK universities, often driven by 'voluntary severance schemes' that tend to be divisive and can undercut union bargaining power. Although the manifestos generally promote a reinstatement of the core values and purpose of higher education as the central mandate of universities (e.g. Halffman & Radder 2015), there is little evidence that the precarious *research* workforce (as opposed to the teaching precariat) has been considered. In more than one case, redundancies in the UK were coupled with a pledge by the university to invest in additional fixed-term contract researchers, causing tensions between academic and research staff and making contract researchers unwittingly complicit in advancing the conditions that shaped their precarious employment in the first place. It is vital that this kind of divisiveness is combatted both by universities and the precariat (Standing 2011).

The National Tertiary Education Union in Australia has undertaken campaigns over recent years and has a fee structure that accommodates casual workers based on a sliding income scale, including a nominal annual fee for unemployed researchers. The union has advocated for casual academics, informing tenured staff of the various issues associated with the plight of their non-tenured colleagues; and has worked with casual staff on industrial issues (e.g. Nanda 2018). The University of Queensland has a Charter of Rights for Casual Academic Staff (Clifton 2019) that also calls for recognition, representation and improved working conditions for all casual academics, including those in the research workforce.

In the US, the Service Employees International Union's *Adjunct Action* is described as a movement in which 'faculty, graduate student workers, students and families are coming together for change' (http://seiufacultyforward.org/). Members have collectively taken a range of actions from arguing for political change through discussions with US presidential candidates (for the 2020 election) to lobbying for the rights of graduate student researchers to collectivise.

There are anecdotal instances of researchers challenging their conditions, for example, in Japan, where a researcher sued her university for reinstatement and back wages after a non-renewal of a research contract (Okunuki 2014). In her statement after the verdict (where she received an additional one-year contract but no backpay) she said:

> Although the number of irregular, casual and contingent workers is skyrocketing at universities around the country, most researchers just roll over when subjected to injustice because of the fear of the impact any dispute would have on future job prospects. To those part-time teachers who constantly face the crisis of nonrenewal, I want to say that nothing will change unless we raise our voices. More importantly, something might change if we do raise our voices. Nothing would give me more pleasure than if even one more person gained courage from knowing about my case.

Research associations

There is some evidence that research associations are beginning to understand the significant role they might play in advocating for and supporting contract researchers. Levels of concrete support, however, vary greatly. Examples include providing reduced rates for professional memberships for contract researchers, providing discounted conference fees and scholarships, and advocating for fairer conditions. While the majority of associations have introduced some or all of these measures for research students, and many have emeritus benefits, there are relatively few examples of support for post-doctoral and/or contract researchers. Some examples of initiatives that research associations are undertaking include:

- The Australian Sociological Association (TASA) now has a fee structure based on annual income. (https://tasa.org.au/membership/).
- The British Sociological Association (BSA) offers a reduced fee for early career researchers, defined as being within three years of PhD completion. The BSA are also one of several associations to offer reductions for individuals in middle- and low-income countries (www.britsoc.co.uk/membership/membership-categories-rates/).
- The American Historical Association (2018) gives preference to doctoral students nearing completion, non-tenured academics and unaffiliated researchers in awarding grants and fellowship funding (www.historians.org/awards-and-grants/grants-and-fellowships).
- The British Education Research Association (BERA) operates an Early Career Researcher network that aims to 'provide opportunities for early career researchers to engage with their peers to develop their knowledge and skills; to gain experience and to network; and to be connected with BERA and the broader academic community within education' (www.bera.ac.uk/community/early-career-researcher-network).

Although these examples provide positive instances of progress, they are far from the norm, and we are unable to say that contract researchers are well represented by research associations. The inequitable nature of membership to research associations can be compounded by the fact that conferences are one of the main activities of associations, and, as we explored in Chapter 2, opportunities to attend conferences are much more limited for contract researchers than their tenured colleagues.

The impact of institutional initiatives

> Under New Public Management, the proportionately dwindling number of tenured or core academics is subjected to more and more control to ensure compliance with institutional performance measures. Conversely, the increasing number of casual academics is largely ignored, despite their contribution to the teaching function of the university.
>
> (Ryan et al. 2017, p. 58)

Universities and other research organisations are beginning to acknowledge some of the problems associated with temporary research careers and take measures to improve them. Where there are policies or principles that seek to grapple with these issues (e.g. the *Researcher Concordat* and Vitae Projects in the UK) their enactment within organisations is often patchy. As the *Fairweather* example (see Vignette 3.3) showed, even when institutions establish policies and programs with the very best of intentions, implementation may lack formal monitoring and rely on the goodwill of individuals. Equally, there is often very little involvement of researchers themselves in implementation, steering or monitoring these initiatives. Where casual researchers are involved in developing, implementing and evaluating these initiatives, their contributions generally form part of their unpaid workload.

In the US, an increasing number of universities are reviewing policies and practices for the employment of non-tenure track academics. California State University, Dominguez Hills, for example, has created opportunities for non-tenure track faculty to apply for sabbaticals, research funding, awards and advancement into multi-year contracts (CSUDH 2018; Kezar 2018). The CSU program also includes non-tenured employees on various committees. These changes emerged from a *Task Force to Recommend Best Practices for Non-Tenure-Track Instructional Faculty* (2018), which undertook significant research into contract work and delivered a set of comprehensive recommendations in 2018. Similarly, Austin Peay State University has proposed the establishment of a Centre for Adjunct Faculty Support & Engagement (CASE) to 'implement best practices available at other institutions of higher education to support our fellow adjunct faculty' (Chester-Fangman et al. 2018, p. 1).

Many institutions in the UK publish action plans pertaining to work on implementing the *Researcher Concordat* (e.g. University of Oxford 2011) to address some of these challenges. Individual organisations have developed instances of good institutional practice. In the UK, a study was conducted in Lancaster University's Faculty of Health and Medicine, for example, to investigate employment conditions and experiences of their contract researchers with the aim of improving practices, support and career development for them (Brown et al. 2017).

The importance of supportive management goes beyond helping researchers become better researchers, it is about generating and building collective capacity for the development of research and education. As demonstrated through the *Fairweather* example (Vignette 3.3), however, this capacity can be undermined by the temporary conditions under which researchers work, leading to a cyclical production of work, learning and loss creating institutional and research amnesia. Loss of researchers with valuable expertise and networks compromises organisational memory and the capacity to learn and build on collective knowledge. Inconsistency in research teams can limit researchers in building long-term programs of research and lead to more fragmented approaches.

The researchers we talked to in assembling this book often had their own views on how *institutions* could best support them and harness their capacity. Amelia said of the universities she has worked at:

> There's no leadership plan here, there's no sense of grooming your HDRs[4] to bring them in, to build on that knowledge, to build your capacity, your research capacity. Why would you invest all that time and effort in developing research capacity in somebody and then send them out the door? And they take that research and go elsewhere. I just cannot understand it.

As Nadolny and Ryan (2015) point out, even organisations like McDonald's compare favourably with universities in terms of many labour practices. Contract researchers are not only expected to undertake unpaid training (if it is available at all) and manage their own career progression, but might find themselves 'locked-in' to insecure work in universities. Work in academia is often perceived as being high status and valuable through the enduring view of the 'ivory tower'. Yet as the accounts in Chapters 2 and 3 highlight, a more accurate description is that much of the research work was conducted in an 'ivory basement' (in which research and professional staff are employed without the same support as permanent academic staff (Eveline & Booth 2004)).

Impacts on universities

Goode (2006, p. 1) argues that:

> there is a paradox ... in the way that contract researchers accrue a wealth of experience of how research is organized and conducted in different contexts, a repertoire of skills, and a vast volume of various kinds of data, while remaining vulnerable and marginalized figures within the academy, with few opportunities for professional development and advancement.

Quite apart from the instability, incoherence and injustice experienced by vast and increasing numbers of employees, the system of casualised employment of the research and teaching workforce is destructive for the core purpose and values associated with universities: research and education. As the 'slow academic' movement suggests, the accelerated pace of academic work can compromise the quality that has traditionally been associated with deep, sustained programs of work and the wellbeing of the academic workforce (Berg & Seeber 2016).

There is a clear paradox in that the reliance on contract research positions allows the university to limit economic risk while increasing the workforce available to produce research outcomes (through publications and grants) but could limit the depth of this research and the intellectual capital of the institution as a whole. One practical example of this paradox can be found in the lack of support for capacity building that we find for contract researchers— in spite of the fact that contract researchers bring vital intellectual capital and build capacity for their organisations, and more broadly contribute to the production of knowledge, Andrea indicates:

> To me, I think the thing that I find most incredible is that, you know, to my mind, anybody who is working there is not going to stay there. Simple as that. So you lose, you know, I've just gone through the corporate review and you have, you know, you can see more broadly across tertiary education that building capacity is one of the biggest things. Research capacity, but also leadership capacity, and not just generally, but from a gender perspective, from an Indigenous perspective, these are just not things you can just turn around like that. You need to have planning in place.
>
> It just seems to me an awful waste of opportunity. You've the opportunity to identify, continue to build on your point of difference in the market. You know, not only for higher degree research students coming in, but for undergraduates, to be saying to your undergraduates, "You're going to be taught by experts in your field.". Some of those people might have been experts now. Who steps into their shoes when they go? I don't know. I just don't understand. I just don't understand.

Fixed-term contracts can create unstable working environments that limit universities' ability to capitalise on their knowledge workers, which impact on research quality and productivity (Lafuente & Berbegal-Mirabent 2017). While we have already called attention to challenges faced by contract researchers with regards to writing, co-authoring and publishing research (see Chapters 2 and 3), this is far more than an individual struggle. Publications are widely accepted as a key metric for individual and institutional productivity and success. Therefore, while they are essential for individual academic career advancement, they are also central to the collective production and exchange of knowledge and, under the current evaluative regimes of several advanced liberal economies, to the financial security of the institution.

Another issue to which we have drawn attention (see Chapter 2) is whether present practices support rigorous and ethical research. Ethics and rigour are two of the core values associated with the 'higher' purpose of research. Yet, many of the individuals with whom we talked, had experienced an uncomfortable disjuncture between their concept of quality research and the tasks required in their work. Some of our participants found meaning in the attempt to maintain their own commitments in the face of this confrontation but this might also expose them to a variety of risks including risks associated with job insecurity. Jill, for example, had watched a Chief Investigator on her project ask contract researchers to delete research data. Becoming aware of this issue, Jill decided that the research data should be preserved, despite the lead researchers' instructions and so decided to make a copy on her computer at the university:

> so before he deleted all that, I just copied it
> ... And thank God I did because ... I had to

> come back for on [another] short-term contract ... It was like a whole retrospective of the seven-year project and thank God I had kept all those files there, because—hey! He had deleted them and then he used to work on USBs. Those USBs would fold ...

Jill said that she felt 'a little bit of guilt there' but that ultimately she had decided that 'this is way it should be done'. This pattern of behaviour led Jill to adopt a strategy of retaining files of other casual researchers before they left the project. She said, 'I had to keep evidence and mark it and date it and [record] who's who, so if an issue came up and he'd accuse me of doing something I could then say, "well, no. Here's the history trail"'.

These accounts signal the need for universities to develop a better understanding of their insecurely employed researchers, because, as they reveal, contract researchers often have a deep understanding of research practices, and compliance with university and public ethical standards and expectations. If universities and other research organisations are to continue to lay claim to public values of research and education, then they must work to address these concerns. Put simply, if the employment practices of universities and other research organisations undermine the conduct of rigorous and ethical research, then what is the purpose of these organisations?

Government-led reform

Although institutional principles and policies sometimes promote greater inclusion of contract researchers, there is often a distinct mismatch between the spirit of such policies and their realisation in practice. This is in part a critique of universities and other research organisations, but also a critique of the broader structures according to which it 'makes sense' for the research workforce to be organised as it currently is.

Universities and other research organisations frequently allude to the difficulties of doing anything differently when they are collectively so dependent on temporary funding streams. Accordingly, the rationale is that it 'makes sense' to organise the research workforce according to temporary contracts. Research councils and other funders therefore hold substantial power. With this power should come a greater responsibility and more concrete commitment to the long-term needs of the research workforce. While contract research is a large and complex problem, relatively simple strategies exist for improvement. For example, councils and funders could collectively agree to increase the proportion of programme funding relative to project funding. Programmes tend to be longer than projects, and often have a broader remit than individual projects. Funders could build in formal requirements related to community and capacity building as conditions of funding and monitor these in the same way they monitor other outcomes and outputs. One example might be setting quotas on minimum contract lengths and imposing limits on the use of casual employment within programmes.

There is a great raft of other possible initiatives that could come from the top down. For example, the same kind of incentives that have been introduced to evaluative regimes to promote both recruitment and completion rates for PhD students could be used to support the needs and interests of post-doctoral researchers. There has been a good deal of progress in some countries in mapping out a career structure and trajectory for contract researchers. The government sponsored *Vitae Project* in the UK, sets out a researcher development framework. An increasing number of universities are adopting these frameworks or using them to set out standardised criteria for career progression and advancement that are more relevant to both the tasks and aspirations of research-only positions. However, such initiatives generally lack a corresponding shift in the creation of conditions that might support the contract research workforce as a whole to move towards the attainment of these criteria. This means that researchers wishing to advance will need to demonstrate not only that they have done the jobs for which they are contracted, but also that they have achieved milestones related to things like impact, professional service and leadership, things for which they might not be formally contracted or have had to undertake invisible and unpaid work.

A final word

> For me, part of the academic pleasure is the creative spaces of pleasure, which is all about I'd define it as being about cognition, challenge and choice, and if you perceive yourself as 'contract researcher' who's doing the donkey work, so you're not really having to think that hard, it's all pretty basic, there's no real challenge to it, you know how to do it, and there's no real choice, you've been assigned it, then that's the entire creative pleasure of being an academic, it's not there.
>
> —Helen Sword

Responses to precarity in research, particularly within the academic workforce are not easy, and it is unlikely that this 'fragmented, casualised "gig economy"' (Richardson & Heffernan 2019) will dissipate anytime soon. Growing attention on the impact of this work, however, suggests that there is a movement that is starting to redefine these issues as institutional, systemic problems rather than simply problems for the individuals involved. We cited Raewyn Connell early in this book, illustrating our belief that the insecurity of contract research is not, and should not be seen as a personal issue but as an issue that needs to be addressed collectively. By moving these discussions out of the corridors and into the public sphere, we are hoping to provoke more consideration of alternative strategies to support all researchers working in precarious spaces. While we have offered some suggestions for how researchers can develop ethical, cooperative strategies to support one another under current conditions, we argue that there is a need for greater change but are unsure of what guise that might take. As one Vice Chancellor (cited by Andrews et al. 2016, p. 17) stated when asked about changing conditions in relation to casual employment, however:

> the solutions will not be simple and there will be trade-offs. But, as with most things in life, the fact that the path is uncertain should not stop us from walking it.

Notes

1 Research Exercise Framework—the principal means through which university research is quality assessed in the UK; www.ref.ac.uk
2 www.ucu.org.uk/free
3 www.ucu.org.uk/stampout
4 Higher Degree Research Students.

References

American Historical Association, 2018, *AHA Grants and Fellowships*, www.historians.org/awards-and-grants/grants-and-fellowships, accessed 3 August 2019.

Andrews, S., Bare, L., Bentley, P., Goedegebuure, L., Pugsley, C. & Rance, B., 2016, *Contingent Academic Employment in Australian Universities*, Melbourne: LH Martin Institute and the Australian Higher Education Industrial Association, www.lhmartininstitute.edu.au/documents/publications/2016-contingent-academic-employment-in-australian-universities-updatedapr16.pdf, accessed 7 March 2018.

Archer, J., Pajo, K. & Lee, L., 2018, 'Perceptions of precariousness and employment strain: The role of the manager', in *Proceedings of the Australia and New Zealand Academy of Management Annual Conference*, www.anzam.org/wp-content/uploads/pdf-manager/94_ANZAM-2013-202.PDF, accessed 30 August 2019.

Bain, P.G., Mann, L. & Pirola-Merlo, A., 2001, 'The innovation imperative: The relationships between team climate, innovation, and performance in research and development teams', *Small Group Research*, vol. 32, no. 1, pp. 55–73.

Berg, M. & Seeber, B.K., 2016, *The Slow Professor: Challenging the Culture of Speed in the Academy*, Toronto: University of Toronto Press.

Bone, K., Jack, G. & Mayson, S., 2018, 'Negotiating the greedy institution: A typology of the lived experiences of young, precarious academic workers', *Labour & Industry: A Journal of the Social and Economic Relations of Work*, vol. 28, no. 4, pp. 225–243, doi: 10.1080/10301763.2018.1528654.

Brown, J., Shaw, E., Pickup, R. & Morbey, H., 2017, *Contract Researcher Audit and Survey–Foundation Report January 2017*, University of Lancaster: Faculty of Health & Medicine, Lancaster University, www.lancaster.ac.uk/users/ucu/campaigns/RCAD%20Survey%20Summary%20(Visual%20Version).pdf, accessed 25 August 2019.

California State University, Dominguez Hills (CSUDH), 2018, *Report of the Task Force to Recommend Best Practices for Non-Tenure-Track Instructional Faculty*, www.csudh.edu/Assets/csudh-sites/president/docs/task-force/FINAL-REPORT-Non-Tenure-Track-Faculty-Task-Force.pdf, accessed 9 March 2018.

Carrigan, M. & Vostal, F., 2016, 'Not so fast! A critique of the slow professor', *University Affairs*, www.universityaffairs.ca/opinion/in-my-opinion/not-so-fast-a-critique-of-the-slow-professor/, accessed 30 July 2019.

Chester-Fangman, C., Hooper, M., Hunt, K., Markov, S. & Truhon, S., 2018, 'Beyond Pay! Making the CASE for success: Implementing a Center for Adjunct Support & Engagement at Austin Peay State University', PhD thesis, Tennessee, Austin Peay State University, https://pdfs.semanticscholar.org/bc67/2fbdec4451e2e77bf313f70f-86655416de3d.pdf, accessed 24 August 2019.

Clifton, P., 2019, 'UQ charter of rights for casual academic staff', *Connect, National Tertiary Education Union*, vol .12, no. 1, www.unicasual.org.au/article/UQ-Charter-of-Rights-for-Casual-Academic-Staff-%28Connect-12-01%29-21295, accessed 25 August 2019.

Dowland, D. & Pérez, A., 2018, *How to be a Generous Professor in Precarious Times*, www.chronicle.com/article/How-to-Be-a-Generous-Professor/244581, accessed 25 August 2019.

Eveline, J. & Booth, M., 2004, '"Don't write about it" Writing 'the other' for the ivory basement', *Journal of Organizational Change Management*, vol. 17, no. 3, pp. 243–255.

Goode, J., 2006, 'Research identities: Reflections of a contract researcher', *Sociological Research Online*, vol. 11, no. 2, pp. 1–13.

Halffman, W. & Radder, H., 2015, 'The academic manifesto: From an occupied to a public university', *Minerva*, vol. 53, no. 2, pp. 165–187.

Kezar, A., 2018, 'Hope for faculty off the tenure track?' *Inside Higher Education*, www.insidehighered.com/views/2019/05/28/institutions-should-learn-some-good-examples-how-support-adjunct-faculty-opinion, accessed 24 August 2019.

Lafuente, E. & Berbegal-Mirabent, J., 2017, 'Contract employment policy and research productivity of knowledge workers: An analysis of Spanish universities', *The International Journal of Human Resource Management*, vol. 30, no. 16, pp. 2360–2386, doi: 10.1080/09585192.2017.1323226.

Mendick, H., 2014, 'Social class, gender and the pace of academic life: What kind of solution is slow?', *Forum Qualitative Sozialforschung/Forum: Qualitative Social Research*, vol. 15, no. 3, doi: http://dx.doi.org/10.17169/fqs-15.3.2224.

Nadolny, A. & Ryan, S., 2015, 'McUniversities revisited: A comparison of university and McDonald's casual employee experiences in Australia', *Studies in Higher Education*, vol. 40, no. 1, pp. 142–157.

Nanda, G., 2018, 'I pledge' campaign', *Connect, National Tertiary Education Union*, vol .12, no. 1, https://issuu.com/nteu/docs/connect_12_01, accessed 25 August 2019.

Okunuki, H., 2014, 'Job insecurity among Japan's university teachers is a recipe for further decline', *Japan Times*. www.japantimes.co.jp/community/2014/09/24/issues/job-insecurity-among-japans-university-teachers-recipe-decline/#.XWCh8pMzaL8, accessed 25 August 2019.

Percy, A., Scoufis, M., Parry, S., Goody, A. & Hicks, M., 2008, *The RED Report, Recognition – Enhancement – Development: The Contribution of Sessional Teachers to Higher Education*, Sydney: Australian Learning and Teaching Council.

Richardson, P. & Heffernan, A., 2019, 'Our university workforce has become a fragmented, casualised 'gig economy', The problems we face', *AARE EduResearch Matters: A Voice for Australian Educational Researchers*, www.aare.edu.au/blog/?p=4087, accessed 4 July 2019.

Ryan, S., Burgess, J., Connell, J. & Groen, E., 2013, 'Casual academic staff in an Australian university: Marginalised and excluded', *Tertiary Education and Management*, vol. 19, no. 2, pp. 161–175, doi: 10.1080/13583883.2013.783617.

Ryan, S., Connell, J. & Burgess, J., 2017, 'Casual academics: A new public management paradox', *Labour & Industry: A Journal of the Social and Economic Relations of Work*, vol. 27, no. 1, pp. 56–72.

Scott, S., 2019, 'Focus: Inequalities in the academy: Cogs in search of a new wheel', *Discover Society*, https://discoversociety.org/2019/07/03/focus-inequalities-in-the-academy-cogs-in-search-of-a-new-wheel/, accessed 27 July 2018.

Standing, G., 2011, *The Precariat – The New Dangerous Class*, London: Bloomsbury.

Starratt, R.J., 2012, *Cultivating an Ethical School*, New York: Routledge.

Starratt, R.J., 2014, 'Ethics and social justice: Strangers passing in the night?', in I Bogotch and CM Shields (eds), *International Handbook of Educational Leadership and Social (In) Justice*, New York: Springer, pp. 67–80.

Sue, D.W., 2010, 'Microaggressions marginality and oppression', in DW Sue; (ed), *Microaggressions and Marginality: Manifestation, Dynamics, and Impact*, Hoboken: John Wiley & Sons, pp. 3–24.

University of Oxford, 2011, *University of Oxford Concordat to Support the Career Development of Research Staff: European Commission HR Excellence in Research Badge Gap Analysis and Action Plan*, www.admin.ox.ac.uk/media/global/wwwadminoxacuk/localsites/personnel/documents/informationforstaff/HR_excellence_in_research_badge_action_plan_oct_2011.pdf, accessed 25 August 2019.

Index

'Academic Diary' (Back, 2016) 1
academic labour 45
accountability for work 108, 122–123
adaptability as key characteristic 105, 107
additional hours, working 118, 123, 134, 169; *see also* unpaid work
adjunct faculty 18, 20, 141, 164–165
administration, university 37–38, 62–65, 169
administrative contracts: moving from research into 91–92; as route to research jobs 41–43
administrative tasks of research work 116–117
advertised posts 40, 88–90, 95, 128–129
age of contract researchers 18, 79–86
ageing 78–86
alienation 46
Allan, K. 45
Allen-Collinson, J. 15, 106
Altmetrics 55
Alvesson, M. 57

American Historical Association 180
American Mathematical Society 124
Andrews, S. 5, 15, 19, 25, 27, 183
Angervall, P. 17
anxiety 77, 90, 91, 144
applying for jobs 72–73, 88–90, 93
apprenticeship phase 15, 18, 28; *see also* pseudo-probationary period
Archer, J. 160–161
Association of University Teachers report (Bryson & Tulle-Winton 1994) 26
attrition (leaving research work) 29, 47, 125, 176, 178
Austin Peay State University 175
Australia: advertised posts 40, 88–89; casual contracts 6; fixed-term contracts 15; funding 14; increased student numbers 5; mobility 130–131; policy context 22; research-only roles 19; sessional lecturers 18;

Index

unions 171; Work for the Dole 82–83
Australian Research Council 22
Australian Sociological Association (TASA) 173
authorship questions 121–126
auto-ethnographic accounts 14
autonomy 38, 47, 110

Back, Les 1–2
Bain, P.G. 166
Ball, Stephen 8, 71
Baranay, I. 68
Barcan, R. 4
Barnes, N. 103
belonging, feelings of 114–115
Berbegal-Mirabent, J. 179
Berg, M. 156, 177
Bexley, E. 17
bid-writing 27; see also grant-writing
Blackwell, R. 26
Bone, K. 161
Booth, M. 17, 28, 177
Bosanquet, A. 18, 79
Boulos, A. 14
boundaryless careers 30
Bourdieu, P. 48, 57
Bourne, H.R. 14
Bozeman, B. 23
Brady, M. 25, 26, 27, 28, 29
Briody, R. 25, 26, 27, 28, 29
British Education Research Association (BERA) 180
British Sociological Association (BSA) 173
Broadbent, K. 27, 28, 103
Bröckling, U. 52

Brown, J. 17, 175
Brown, T. 26, 28, 58
Bryson, C. 26, 103
budget management skills 59
bullying 46, 111, 143
burnout 81; see also stress
business values 24

Cadambi, D.M. 15
California State University, Dominguez Hills 175
Canada 13, 18
Cannizzo, F. 45
capacity building 176–178, 181
career breaks 22
career progression: access to career-building skills 27; collective work of career building 127–144; future possibilities for 166, 178; government-led reform 180–182; little evidence of 26; policy context 22–24; strategic career planning 49–55, 140
Carrigan, M. 156
casual contracts, definition 6
casualisation as a general trend 25–26, 29, 163, 170
Centre for Adjunct Faculty Support & Engagement (CASE) 175
characteristics of successful contract researchers 104–110
Chester-Fangman, C. 175
children 17, 77
Christmas 76
Clance, P.R. 48
Clarke, C.A. 114

Clarke, Teena 167–170
Cochran-Smith, M. 51
Coin, F. 45
cold calling 40, 52
collaborative research 61, 97
collaborative strategies 102–153
collective solutions 7–9, 81, 102–153, 158–160, 183
collectivisation 144–150
Commonwealth Scientific and Industrial Research Organisation (CSIRO) 14
communication with other researchers 61–62; see also networks
community spirit (lack of) 135
competitive processes 40, 55–56, 95, 103, 141–142
computer log-in issues 37
Concordat Consultation Report (Concordat Strategy Group 2019) 23
Concordat to Support the Career Development of Researchers (UKRI 2008) 22–23, 174, 175
conference attendance 102–103, 106, 134, 139–141, 161, 180
confidence 91, 97, 108
connecting jobs together 50, 53–54
Connell, Professor Raewyn 7–8, 19, 93, 159, 165–166, 183
contacts, building 52–53, 127–139; see also networks
contingent faculty 4–5, 15
continuity of employment 47, 72–73, 95

control, lack of 105, 107, 111–112
corporatisation of academia 24–26
costs of employment, seeking to reduce 24–25
Courtois, A. 16, 26, 28
cover for permanent staff 26
critical friend roles 154–155
critique, ethic of 164
Crossouard, B. 13
CVs 54, 89, 92

data (from research projects), issues with publishing 117–118, 179
data (on contract research), lack of accurate 19–22, 23
deadlines, meeting 70
death insurance 80
definition of *making it* 2–4, 150, 155–156
definitions, key 6, 12–13, 150
de-legitimisation 46
demographics of contract researchers 17–18; see also age of contract researchers; gender
denizens 16
desk space 46, 114
Deuchar, R. 104
disability 131
disconnection 1, 28, 160
disempowerment 46
Dowland, D. 165

early career researchers 18–19, 23, 49–50, 88, 127, 154, 173, 180
early retirement 84–85
editorial work 123
Edwards, D. 43

email lists, exclusion from 46, 115
emotional labour 108, 122
entrepreneurial skills 43, 52, 57, 104
entry to contract research 38–43
equality of entitlements 81
estimating time taken 68
ethical colleagues 94–98, 121, 126, 142–144, 160–170
ethical dilemmas 111–113
ethical research 179–180
ethical supervision 78–79, 121, 160–170
ethnicity 131
European Commission 25–26
European University Institute 3
Eurostat 26
Eveline, J. 17, 28, 177
everyday experiences 5, 9, 12
exiting precarious work 28
expectations, mismatches of 87–88, 90, 109
experience, gathering 14, 39–40, 49–50, 96–97, 105–106, 130
expertise, developing an area of 50–51, 96–98, 105, 130
exploitation 26, 94; *see also* additional hours; unpaid work

faculty events 134
Fairweather Researcher Group 145–150, 174, 175
'falling into' contract research 38–39
family responsibilities 77, 78, 130–131, 164
feedback 110
feminist scholarship 17–18, 45
finances: balancing timing of contracts 74–76; budget management skills 59; charging fairly for your work 68–72; complex requirements for receiving 64–65; conference attendance 140–141; costs of employment 37; delays 64; and the ethic of justice 163–164; low pay/status 26; part-time incomes 119–120; pensions xi; unemployment gaps 73–77; working more hours than paid for 68; *see also* unpaid work
finding new work 46, 72–74, 95, 127–131, 147
Finland 13
first author status 124, 125–126
fixed-term contracts: and the costs of employment 24–25; creation of unstable working environments 179; definition 6, 21; disadvantage experienced by contract researchers 27; statistics on 15–16; transaction-based relationship 119
Flaherty, C. 4–5

flexibility as key characteristic 105, 106
flexible working 79, 87
Floersch, J. 6
free, working for 44–45, 48, 56, 118–120; *see also* unpaid work
freeway flyers 75
FTE (full-time-equivalent) reporting 19
Fumasoli, T. 89, 129
funding: changes in government funding 14–15, 25, 181; for professional training 58–59; and short-term work 75; soft money 14, 15, 25, 94; tethering to measurement frameworks 22; writing proposals for 27
future work, securing 46, 72–73, 89–90, 95, 161

gaps between contracts 673–78
Gaughan, M. 23
gender: authorship questions 124; contract researchers predominantly female 17–18; and the ethic of justice 163–164; and geographical mobility 131; labours of love 45
geographical displacement 27, 78, 130–131
Georghiou, L. 4
Giddens, A. 47
Gill, R. 120
goal setting 49–51
Goastellec, G. 89, 129
good performance 25

Goode, J. 177
Göttingen/Humboldt model of universities 15
government funding 14, 25, 181
government-led reform 180–182
grants 24, 25
grant-writing 27, 59, 60, 146–147
Green, A.E. 105
Gregg, M. 45
growth of contract research 13–17
Gruber, T. 55

Halffman, W. 171
Hardy-Littlewood Rule 124
Harney, B. 27, 30, 69, 103
Harris, J. 94–98
Hayot, E. 69
health issues 78–86, 131
Heffernan, A. 12, 183
Herschberg, C. 128
Hey, V. 17, 105, 106
hidden work 62–86, 150, 159–160, 182
hierarchies 17, 45, 48
Higher Education Chronicle 164
Higher Education Funding Council for England 18
Hill, D. 15
Hockey, J. 15, 106
holiday leave 62, 76–77
Holligan, C. 108, 110
home, working from 114, 133, 135
hope labour 45
Hopwood, Nick 168
hot-desking 114
hourly-paid staff 19
Howard, B. 14

identity: and anxiety about the next job 77; career identities 17; developing an academic identity 44–49, 51, 57, 72–73, 104, 116; impact of applying for jobs on 90; imposter syndrome 48, 69, 96, 114–115; lack of secure work-based 17; working unpaid to develop 119–120
Imes, S.A. 48
immigration requirements 67
impact measurement 25, 156
imposter syndrome 48, 69, 96, 114–115, 144
in kind support 144
in-demand skills 57–60
independently, ability to work 109–110
industrial action 170–172
industry-funded research 117–118
inequality of opportunity 26, 164
inequity 24
informal networks 128–131, 135, 136
informed consent 113
insider perspectives 5
Institute of Medicine 13, 15, 18
institutional initiatives 172–179
insurance 80
intellectual capital 105, 178
intellectual property 117–118
intensification of academic work 3, 120, 133

International Committee of Medical Journal Editors (ICMJE) 122
invisibility 28, 62–86, 150, 159–160, 182
Ireland 15, 17
isolation 26, 133, 159
Italy 45, 128
Ivancheva, M.P. 17, 27, 56, 69
ivory basement 17, 175

Japan 172
job applications 72–73, 88–91, 93
Journal Citation Reports 55
justice 163–164

Kamler, B. 44
Kezar, A. 175
Kimber, M. 28, 95
Knights, D. 114
knowledge producers, contract researchers as 93, 179

labour of love 45
Lafuente, E. 179
Lancaster University 175
lead researchers 61, 76, 105, 118, 163, 166, 179
leading on publications 125–126
leave entitlements 62, 76–77, 164
leaving academia 29
leaving research work (attrition) 29, 47, 176, 178
Lee, Alison 168
liberalism 8, 9, 13, 24–25, 90
limiting use of casual employment 181

line management 66, 146, 155, 160, 161, 163, 167
literature review work 20, 69, 70, 71, 116, 118
lock-in 176
long hours, working 8, 72, 75, 88, 95, 123
Loveday, V. 90, 115
Lynch-Biniek, A. 75
Lynda.com 59

Macfarlane, B. 4, 121
Management of researchers 8, 162–163, 175; *see also* line management; supervisors
managerialism 24–26
marginalisation of contract researchers 28, 159–160, 177
marketisation of higher education 4
Maroudas, E. 4, 71
Marriott, J. 135
massification of higher education 4, 13, 15, 114
maternity leave 78
Maxwell, N. 17
McCulloch, S. 106
McDonald, T. 17
McDonald's 58, 63, 176
Mendick, H. 130, 156
Mensitieri, G. 25, 48
mentoring 93, 97, 121, 135, 136, 137, 154, 161
Mewburn, Inger 40, 51, 88, 92
Milojević, S. 29
Mingers, J. 24
minimum contract lengths 149, 181
miscommunication 61–62

mission statements 51
mobility (geographical) 27, 78, 130–131
motherhood penalty 17
moving beyond contract research 86–93
multi-institution affiliations 37–38
multiple (contemporaneous) contracts 37–38, 63, 95, 168
multiple successive temporary contracts 27–28; *see also* continuity of employment
multi-talented academics 88–90; *see also* superheroes

Nadolny, A. 4, 24, 29, 58, 63, 176
narrative, building a 49–55
National Tertiary Education Union 171
neoliberalism 4–5, 8, 155, 156, 167, 178
networks: building networks of contacts 52–53, 127–131, 139–141, 161, 173; of contract researchers 141–144; sustaining 131–139
neurotic academics 90
New Public Management 174
new work, finding 46, 72–74, 95, 127–131, 147
New Zealand 5, 160
niches, finding your 49
Nikolaidis, E. 4, 71
non-academic research work 14

non-PhD holders 41–42
non-research work, combining with 75–76
non-research work, moving to 91–93
non-standard hours 68
Nuutinen, A. 13

Oakley, A. 17
office space 37, 46, 114
O'Keefe, T. 16, 26, 28
Okunuki, H. 172
older researchers 18, 79–86
on-the-job training 58–59, 168
ontological insecurity 47, 90
Other, contract researchers as 29
other people's projects, working on 56, 95, 96, 97, 104–126
outputs, measurement of 24, 70
overcrowded workspaces 114
oversupply of graduates/PhD holders 13, 94

Park, C. 104
part-time contracts 15–16, 19, 119
passion for academic work 45, 48–49, 51
patronage systems 79
payment: charging fairly for your work 68–72; complex requirements for receiving 64; delays 63; working more hours than paid for 68–69; *see also* finances
peer support 147–148; *see also* networks

peers, dealing with 46
pensions xi
Percy, A. 162
Pérez, A. 165
performance metrics: and funding 22; New Public Management 174; number of PhD holders 13–14; and personal development plans 155; publication record 55–57, 116; target-driven regulation 24; *see also* publication
permanent employment: increasingly difficult to get generally 3, 25–26, 86; men more likely in 17; as success criteria 3; traditional expectations of 13, 19
personal branding 51–52
personal development plans 155
Petrova, M. 3
PhD holders: age of commencement 18; employment rates 13; general issues of graduate employment 92–93; non-academic research work 14; oversupply of 13; PhDs as a solo endeavour 104
Pitt, R. 40, 88
Pocock, B. 62
policy context 22–24, 81, 157, 174, 180–181
power relationships: authorship questions 126; contract researchers and employed academics 45–46, 94, 105, 112, 143,

156, 162–163; control over projects 105, 106–107, 111–112; and ethics 113; funders 181; university hierarchies 48
precariat 16–17, 27
prestige 24, 25, 48, 55
privilege 24, 48, 130–131, 163–164
professional associations 179–180
professional development 58–59, 127, 162, 176, 182
professional organisations 139–141, 157, 180
progressing as a contract researcher 43–62
project management approaches 71, 75–76
project-specific grants 14
pseudo-probationary period 28
psychological contract 86–87, 119–120
publication: authorship questions 97, 121–125; building a publication track record 55–57, 97, 107, 118–120, 122, 166; collective solutions 146; ethical dilemmas 111; first author status 124, 125–126; getting acknowledgement for writing 115–118; high quality publications 55–56; leading on publications 124–125, 166; as metric 24, 25, 179; *'publish or perish'* 8, 56, 119; team work 125–126; see also writing

quality indicators 24
quality research 3, 8, 24, 55–56, 60–62, 107–112, 179
quantification of research outputs 105, 156
quit lit xii
quota setting 181

race 111, 131
Radder, H. 171
Rea, J. 3
reading 57, 61, 68–70, 71
'real world' impact 25
reciprocal contractual expectations 87
recruitment 40
REF (Research Excellence Framework) 155; see also performance metrics
refusal, politics of 8
research agencies funding 14
research associations 127, 157, 162, 172–173
Researcher Concordat 23–24, 174, 175
researcher development groups 145–150
research-for-hire 47–48, 105
research-only roles 15, 19, 20
responsible researcher, being a 110; see also ethical dilemmas
retail jobs 75–76
retention 29
retirement 15, 79, 80, 81, 84–85
return on investment 4, 45
Richardson, P. 12, 183
rights 16, 72, 81, 115, 170–172

risk transfer 25
Rousseau, D.M. 86–87
Ryan, S. 29, 58, 63, 162, 174, 176

sabbaticals 175
salary sacrifice schemes 80
Sang, K. 68
Sarsons, H. 124
SCImago Journal Rank 55
Scott, Professor Sue 167
Seeber, B.K. 156, 177
seeking work 48, 72–73; *see also* applying for jobs; future work, securing
selection criteria 88–89
self-concept, healthy 121
self-perception 44
self-promotion 72
self-regulation 95, 110
sessional lecturers 18, 20
shame 47, 84
short-term contracts 6, 20–21, 95, 96, 137, 180
short-term funding 14
sick leave 62, 78
Siekkinen, T. 29
skills development: conference attendance 140; in-demand skills 57–60; disadvantage experienced by contract researchers 27; professional development provision 58–59, 127, 162, 177, 182; transferable skills 93, 105
slow academic movement 156, 177
Smith, D.E. 5, 12, 150
social class 28, 130–131
social media 55

soft money 14, 15, 25, 94–95
space to work 114; *see also* office space; working from home
Spicer, A. 57
Spina, N. 94–98
staff meetings 38, 46, 115
Standing, Guy 16, 58, 171
Starratt, R.J. 163
status discord 16
STEM subjects 7, 14
stepping stone, contract research as 39
Strachan, G. 28, 103
strategic career planning 49–55, 139–140
stress 66, 73, 77, 78, 160
strikes x–xi
student loans 22
subjectivities 8, 27, 46, 90
success, concepts of 3
Sue, D.W. 160
Sukhnandan, L. 26
superheroes, requirement to be 73, 88–91, 110, 120
supervisors: building networks 129–130, 134–135, 136; ethical leadership 78–79, 121, 160–170; future of contract research 157; institutional initiatives 173; managing quality research 60–62; patronage systems 79
support groups 154–155
Sword, Helen 42–43, 68, 162, 182

tacit knowledge 144
talent attraction/retention 25, 29

target-driven regulation 24
Task Force to Recommend Best Practices for Non-Tenure-Track Instructional Faculty (CSUDH, 2018) 175
teaching: combining with research 75, 88, 120; effects of casualisation on 29; moving into 91; teaching-only roles 15, 18, 20–21; temporary teaching contracts xi, xiii–xiv; traditional expectations of teaching and research 15
team work 60–62, 104–126, 166–167
temporary employment, general increases in xi–xii
tenuous periphery 95, 98
tenured staff: academic job applications 88–91; and the costs of employment 25; definition 21; divisions between tenured and non-tenured staff 8, 28, 45–46; lack of understanding of contract researchers 159; as lead researchers 105; pressure not to impact 63; traditional expectations of 13; in US 18
tenure-track posts 18
thematic analyses 5–6
Thesis Whisperer website 51
Thomson, Pat xiii, 30, 44, 104, 167
Thornton, M. 17–18
Tight, M. 15
time management 73

time pressures 61–62, 69–70, 71, 113
timesheet completion 62, 63, 64–65, 68, 70
timing of contracts, balancing 74–77
trade unions 170–172
training opportunities 58, 176
transferable skills 93, 105
travel costs 37, 134
travel time 37
Treuthardt, L. 13
tuition fees 22
Tulle-Winton, E. 26
turnover of staff 15
Turok, I. 105
tutoring 52, 91

UK: age of commencement 18; funding 25; number of contract researchers 16; policy context 22–23
UKRI (UK Research and Innovation) 22–23, 26–27
uncertainty, living with 46, 48–49
underclass, creating an 119–120
underemployment, periods of 73–77
underreporting of hours worked 69–72
unemployment gaps 65–66, 73–77, 147
unethical practices 111–113, 126, 179–180
unfair treatment 45–46
unions 170–172
Universities UK 16, 18, 19, 22, 29
University and Colleges Union 19, 26, 29, 170
unpaid training 58–59

unpaid work: to achieve quality research 96; collective solutions 118–120, 175, 182; conference attendance 134; power and privilege 48; publication 56, 116; vocation 44–45
US: adjunct faculty 18; attrition 29; contingent faculty 15; funding 14–15, 25; growth of contract research 13; institutional initiatives 175; policy context 23; tenured staff 4–5; unions 171–172

valued, not feeling 47, 114
visas 65, 66–67
Vitae Project 174, 182
vocation, sense of 44–45
voice 28
Vostal, F. 156

Web of Science 55
Weeden, K.A. 17
wellbeing 115, 143, 155
Willmott, H. 24
Wilson, M. 108, 110

women: authorship questions 123; contract researchers predominantly female 17–18; and the ethic of justice 163–164; and geographical mobility 131
word of mouth 40, 95, 128–129, 168
work, conceptions of 12–13
working from home 114, 135
work-life collision 62
workloads 8, 15, 45, 73, 88, 125, 126
writing: authorship questions 97, 121–125; collective solutions 146; creative process 68; grant-writing 27, 59, 60, 146–147; less time spent on 56; multi-year contracts 70; often done unpaid 118–119; on other people's projects 115–118; pleasures of academic life 57; team work 107; *see also* publication